fa-as

Classics of philosophy and science series, ed. Desmond Clarke

G. W. Leibniz
Discourse on metaphysics
and related writings

G. W. Leibniz
Discourse on metaphysics and related writings

Edited and translated, with an
introduction, notes and glossary, by
R. N. D. Martin *and* **Stuart Brown**

Manchester University Press

Manchester and New York

*Distributed exclusively in the USA and Canada
by* St. Martin's Press Inc.,
175 Fifth Avenue, New York 10010, USA

Copyright © this edition R. N. D. Martin and Stuart Brown 1988

Published by Manchester University Press,
Manchester University Press, Oxford Road,
Manchester, M13 9PL, UK

*Distributed exclusively in the USA and Canada
by* St. Martin's Press Inc.,
175 Fifth Avenue, New York 10010, USA

British Library cataloguing in publication data
  Leibniz, Gottfried Wilhelm
    Discourse on metaphysics and related writings. — (Classics of
    philosophy and science series)
    1. Philosophy
    I. Title II. Martin, R. N. D. III. Brown, Stuart,
    1938– IV. Series V. Discours de metaphysique. *English*
    193 B2572

Library of Congress cataloging in publication data applied for

ISBN 0 7190 2338 6 *hardback*

Typeset in Hong Kong
by Graphicraft Typesetters Ltd

Printed and bound in Great Britain by
Biddles Ltd, Guildford and King's Lynn

Contents

Preface

In preparing this new English edition of Leibniz's *Discourse on Metaphysics* we have sought to make it accessible to students with little or no knowledge of seventeenth-century philosophy. The *Discourse* itself was written for quite a wide range of readers and is less technical and compressed than some of Leibniz's more academic philosophy. But the work is by no means self-explanatory. It assumes a particular intellectual background and a familiarity with a certain terminology. In including an introduction, notes and a glossary, we have tried to supply some understanding of this background and to explain words that are either technical or are used in an unusual sense.

The text itself is one Leibniz was at pains to revise and we have sought to give a full text with all but minor alterations indicated. The text and translation are the subject of a special section below. Here it is sufficient to explain that this is intended to be a good student edition rather than a critical edition.

All the texts are freshly translated and some of the supplementary texts are here translated into English for the first time. It has not been our purpose in choosing these texts, however, to add to the now considerable volume of Leibniz's writings in English. Our purpose has been to choose writings where Leibniz himself amplifies on themes that are touched on more briefly in the *Discourse* itself or where we judged that a comparison with the *Discourse* would be fruitful. We have not sought to complement the *Discourse* with writings that deal with different topics or indicate a significant later development of Leibniz's thought. But we have given references to other works by Leibniz where appropriate.

Any edition of Leibniz's writings that aims to be helpful must run the risk of over-simplification. In the Introduction, where we have most braved this risk, we have added notes that indicate further the basis for what is being said and refer to other relevant literature. We have also included a bibliography at the end with suggestions as to further reading.

The *Discourse* and most of the supplementary texts were originally written in French and R. N. D. Martin was primarily responsible for editing and translating them. Stuart Brown translated the remaining (Latin) texts and was primarily responsible for the introduction, the notes and the glossary. The project has, however, been part of a collaborative study of certain aspects of Leibniz's philosophy from which the mutual benefits have been considerable.

Acknowledgements

We are grateful to the series editor, Dr Desmond Clarke, for encouraging the project and to Dr Clarke, Thomas H. French and Professor G. H. R. Parkinson for comments on draft materials. Professor Dr A. A. Heinekamp and Professor A. Robinet have given us their opinion on certain points to do with the text of the *Discourse*. We are grateful to them, and to the Niedersächsische Landesbibliothek, Hanover, who supplied us with a microfilm of the autograph manuscript. The responsibilitiy for the contents lies entirely with ourselves but we are grateful to Angela Sheffield and Gemma Turner for finding time, amidst the Open University's demanding schedules, to put drafts and corrections on a word processor.

Abbreviations

All references, where possible, have been made the following standard editions of Leibniz's writings, using the following abbreviations:

A   *Leibniz: Sämtliche Schriften und Briefe*, ed. Deutsche Akademie der Wissenschaften, Darmstadt and Leipzig, 1923– (still in progress), followed by the series, volume and page number.

G   *Philosophische Schriften von G. W. Leibniz*, C. I. Gerhardt, 7 vols., Berlin, 1875–90.

GM   *Mathematische Schriften von G. W. Leibniz*, ed. C. I. Gerhardt, 7 vols., Berlin and Halle, 1849–60.

PPL   *Gottfried Wilhelm Leibniz: Philosophical Papers and Letters*, trans. and ed. L. E. Loemker, 2nd Edition, Dordrecht, Holland, D. Reidel, 1969.

Other works referred to in an abbreviated form (most commonly by the name of the author or editor) are cited fully in the bibliography.

The following abbreviations are also used:

Supp.   Supplementary Text, one of twenty pieces of writing related to the *Discourse* and included below.

*   An asterisk is used throughout to indicate a glossary entry under the word that follows.

[.......]   Material deleted or omitted from the final revision of the text.

+........+   Material added in the final revision of the text.

⟨.......⟩ᵃ   Material redrafted in final version (revised version in footnote *a*).

Introduction

1   The history of the *Discourse*

It was not until his fortieth year that Gottfried Leibniz wrote the
work known as the *Discourse on Metaphysics*. He had published
scientific and mathematical articles and already enjoyed some
renown as the inventor of a calculating machine.[1] In the winter of
1685–6, he was engaged on a mining engineering project in the
mines of his Hanoverian masters in the Clausthal-Zellerfield area
of the Harz — an ambitious, though unsuccessful, attempt to use a
system of windmills to improve the drainage system. At the end of
January he was forced, by heavy snowfalls, to take refuge in a
village at the edge of the Harz. It was there that 'having nothing to
do' (*Supp.* 1 below) he drafted his 'short discourse on
metaphysics'.

If his 'discourse' was written quickly, it is nonetheless the
product of many years of thinking about metaphysical questions.
In the previous year or two he had been making a careful study of
a controversy between two leading philosophers of the time,
Nicolas Malebranche and Antoine Arnauld.[2] He had been
reluctant to publish his thoughts on metaphysics, but in 1684 he
wrote an article (*Supp.* 11 below) that partly sought to mediate in
this controversy.

The system that was first expressed in the *Discourse* owes much
to the inspiration of Malebranche. Leibniz once conceded that 'it is
to him that I owe my foundations in this subject' (GM ii 299).
Leibniz admired much in Malebranche's style of philosophical
writing and the *Discourse* is influenced by the form, style and
content of Malebranche's *Treatise of Nature and of Grace*.[3] At the

same time he had an exceptionally high regard for Arnauld's judgement as a critic. In some respects, the *Discourse* may be seen as a critical restatement of a metaphysics not unlike that of Malebranche in which, amongst other things, it was freed from what Leibniz considered to be the valid objections of Arnauld. That is one reason why it may have seemed appropriate to Leibniz to seek Arnauld's opinion of a draft of the work.

Leibniz had met both Malebranche and Arnauld in Paris during his stay there in the early 1670s. He had shown Arnauld a piece he had written on free will and it seems that Arnauld had formed a very high opinion of Leibniz's promise as a philosopher.[4] Leibniz was, however, a diplomat by profession and his visit to Paris was, at least initially, on business in the service of the Elector of Mainz. Leibniz and his patron, Baron von Boineburg, hoped to avert a war between France and Holland but they arrived in Paris too late. They also hoped to approach Arnauld, a leading member of the *Jansenist sect and a theologian as well as a philosopher of distinction, as a step in furthering a reconciliation between the Catholic and Protestant Churches. This approach was thwarted by the untimely death of Boineburg. Diplomatic niceties seem to have precluded Leibniz taking any initiative on his own account.

It is possible that Leibniz believed that his *Discourse* might serve as a basis for another ecumenical initiative. At all events, his communications about it with Arnauld were all made through a Catholic prince, Count Ernst von Hesse-Rheinfels, who (like Boineburg) was a zealous supporter of Church unity. It was to Hesse-Rheinfels that Leibniz first intimated in February 1686 that he had written what he called 'a short discourse on metaphysics' (see *Supp*. 1). He did not send the draft, perhaps because a clean copy needed to be made, but sent a summary (*Supp*. 2), asking for it to be forwarded to Arnauld for his 'opinion'.

Leibniz paid tribute to Arnauld's excellence as a philosopher but the role he envisaged for him in relation to the *Discourse* was that of a 'censor' (see *Supp*. 1). Arnauld was initially alarmed by what he took to be the fatalistic implications of Leibniz's theses, and it was only once Arnauld had put aside questions of faith that the correspondence between them settled down to a fruitful exchange about philosophical questions. Leibniz won concessions from Arnauld but he can hardly have supposed that Arnauld had eventually given any kind of 'imprimatur' to Leibniz's philosophical theology.[5] At all events Arnauld never saw the full text of the *Discourse* and, though Leibniz later toyed with the idea of publishing it together with his correspondence with Arnauld, he never did so. Leibniz's autograph manuscript was classified with his theological writings under the title *Treatise on the Perfections of God*. The copy taken by his secretary, and later revised in Leibniz's hand, bore no title. It was discovered in a different section of his papers and published in 1846 under the title *Discourse on Metaphysics*, the title by which the work has since been known. It was not until Henri Lestienne's edition of 1907 that the autograph manuscript and the copy were brought together in a critical edition.

The care Leibniz took over revisions and the style of the *Discourse* are among the indications that he intended the work for publication — perhaps for much the same public as Malebranche had successfully reached with his books. At all events, it is written with a keen sense of the philosophical, theological and scientific controversies of the day — controversies of which the twentieth-century reader needs some knowledge in order to appreciate what Leibniz hoped to achieve.

2 The philosophical and religious context

2.1 Innovation and orthodoxy

The philosophers of the seventeenth century that are most often studied today, such as Descartes, Spinoza, Locke and Leibniz, were all 'modern' philosophers. They were consciously breaking away from the style of philosophy that had held sway in the past and continued to hold a dominant place in the curricula of the universities during the seventeenth century.[6] This style of philosophy, known, because it was taught in the 'schools' as 'Scholasticism', was indebted above all to Aristotle and continued to be widely accepted largely because it seemed to be the philosophy most readily reconcilable with orthodox Christianity. Descartes and Malebranche had both sought to present a modern philosophy that was still conducive to orthodox Christianity, but, for rather different reasons in each case, their claims to have preserved orthodoxy were questioned. (see Section 2.2 below).

A major aim of the *Discourse*, indeed, was to present an alternative modern philosophy that would be free of such difficulties. This is one reason why Leibniz makes so much of the 'usefulness' of his own principles 'in matters of piety and religion' (see, e.g. §32).

It is difficult to exaggerate the tense atmosphere which continued to surround any attempt in the second half of the seventeenth century to present new ideas in philosophy that touched at all on matters of religion.[7] Descartes's philosophy continued to be taught by his disciples, known as *Cartesians, but the Scholastic establishment at the Sorbonne continued to press for its suppression. Malebranche, who enjoyed a certain vogue in this period and was the most influential single philosopher until eclipsed by Locke, was eventually to have his books put on the *Index*.[8] Scholasticism remained the dominant philosophy in Germany — Leibniz frequently refers to it as 'the common philosophy' — and his own writings contain much Scholastic jargon (see *Glossary* for examples) as well as having at least the appearance of Scholastic doctrines.[9]

For Scholastics the authority of Aristotle had a place which was traditionally parallel and subordinate to that of the Church. The Church had insisted that its interpretations of Scripture could be doubted only by those who could prove a contrary interpretation. A heavy burden of proof therefore lay with anyone who wished to question ecclesiastical authority. The same was widely taken to apply to intellectual authority generally,[10] and Leibniz made use of a notion of *paradox that conceded to the Scholastics at least a good share, if not a monopoly, of authority in philosophy. Someone who ignored the obligation to give well-authorised opinion its due was known as a 'free-thinker', and someone who put forward new opinions regardless was called an *innovator, a charge that Leibniz (in common with a great many of his contemporaries) was anxious to avoid.

It would be misleading to suggest that there was amongst seventeenth-century philosophers a consensus as to what could be accepted as well-authorised opinion. Common points of reference were already hard to find between Scholastic philosophers and the more extreme forms of modernism represented by the Cartesians. Leibniz found that when addressing his writings to the Scholastics he had to write in a quite different style from what was appropriate when his readers might be Cartesians.[11] In the *Discourse*, where he is addressing both Scholastics and Moderns at the same time, he already seems to assume that each should on some matters be accepted as representing a kind of educated common sense, and on this basis to propose a middle way between the extreme intellectual conservatism of some Scholastics and the ultra-modernism of the Cartesians.

There is no strict equivalent in seventeenth-century philosophy of what, in more democratic times, we would call 'common sense'. But at least some of the statements Leibniz thought he could put forward without further argument and which he thought it would be *paradoxical to deny are those that were later defended as statements of common sense. One such statement is that material bodies are substances, an assumption made throughout the *Discourse* in spite of doubts Leibniz had as to whether it was really true (see §§11 and 34) — doubts he suppressed between the original draft and the later copy, presumably in order to avoid drawing on himself the charge of innovation he was later to make against Berkeley.[12]

The word 'substance' was one extensively used by seventeenth-century philosophers in order to express their individual views about what the world fundamentally consisted of. But it was itself a Scholastic term, and its use by the Moderns involved a variety of extensions whose legitimacy was a matter of continual and confusing debate. Leibniz was by no means alone in thinking that a correct account of substance, if it could be given, would be the key to a correct metaphysics. The central feature of Modern philosophy was, indeed, its rejection of the Scholastic view of substance, in particular the doctrine of *substantial forms.

2.2 *The controversy over substantial forms*
The rejection of Scholasticism by the philosophical *avant-garde* of the seventeenth century has led subsequent writers to exaggerate the coherence of Scholasticism. It would be more true to see it as a language and style of philosophy which provided a framework for debate and, to some extent, a consensus about what the agenda for philosophical debate should be. (The topics touched on by Leibniz in *Discourse* §§30–1 are part of that agenda.)

But even the language and style of philosophy had been called into question as far back as the fourteenth century by the followers of William of Ockham. Long before the seventeenth century there was a recognised distinction between the largely

Aristotelian *via antiqua* and the Ockhamist *via moderna*, with some Universities requiring that both should be taught. All sorts of compromises were made between these two theoretically very different philosophies, and it is doubtful whether Ockham's modernism was often pressed to its logical conclusion before the seventeenth century. But that logical conclusion, once arrived at, was wholly subversive of Aristotelian science, promoting a sceptical view about the possibility of human knowledge of the world.

Central to Aristotelian science was the thought that the world is fundamentally divided into natural kinds; into different sorts of substance each of which has its own distinct essence. The various properties observed in each substance were thought of as deriving from this essence in such a way that anyone who knew that essence would be able to infer, and so explain, these properties. In Aristotelian thought, what was called 'primary matter' was not distinguished into different kinds of substance. What was needed, for such a distinction, was the addition of 'form' to 'matter'. Hence what it was that made one piece of matter into an individual of a particular kind was its 'substantial form'. Individual substances thus enjoyed only a derivative reality as manifestations of the general natures or essences that were the concern of Aristotelian natural philosophy.

Ockhamists denied the existence of such general natures or essences and insisted, on the contrary, that the only realities were individuals. Ockham's razor ('Entities should not be multiplied beyond necessity') was deployed against abstractions like 'essences' and 'substantial forms'. This view became known as 'nominalism' because the Ockhamists denied that there was anything common to that which we call 'apples' (or whatever) beyond the fact that we give certain things the same *name*. ('Nomen' is the Latin for 'name'). But the central point of nominalism as Leibniz understood it, was a thesis about individuals.[13] His own University of Leipzig had been a nominalist stronghold and, perhaps for this reason, Leibniz thought of nominalism as quintessentially 'modern'.

Words like 'new' and 'modern' are, however, confusing because of their time-related character. Leibniz sometimes uses them to refer to nominalism[14] and sometimes to refer to the Modernism of philosophers like Descartes. The distinctively seventeenth-century

Modernism also involved a denial of general natures and substantial forms, but for different reasons. The nub of the objection in this case was that the invocation of such forms failed to explain phenomena and at best merely restated what needed explaining. To take one of Leibniz's examples (*Discourse* §10), it was no good referring to a horodictic quality deriving from the form of a clock to explain how a clock works. Scholastic science came to be thought of as merely obscurantist and by the late seventeenth century the playwright Molière could satirise it through the character of his learned bachelor who explained the fact that opium put people to sleep by its possession of a 'dormitive virtue'.

By reaction against such obscurantism the *mechanical philosophers insisted that explanations should only be given in terms of mathematically intelligible notions, ultimately in terms of size, figure and motion. A main aim of Descartes's metaphysics was to provide an underpinning for this mechanical philosophy. This led him to what was a controversial claim in Leibniz's eyes: that he knew (because he had a 'clear and distinct idea') what the essence of matter was, that matter consisted essentially of extension and its modes (size, figure and motion).[15] Leibniz thought this was claiming too much and, though he accepted that particular phenomena should be explained mechanically so far as possible, he thought that there were limits to the use of mechanical explanations (see, for example, *Discourse* §18).

Leibniz's claimed restoration of substantial forms is linked to his critique of Descartes's account of matter (see *Discourse* §12). A substance, Leibniz supposed, had to have a principle of unity (that made it an individual thing) and principle of identity (that made it the same thing, distinct from other things, at different times). While Descartes was right to abandon substantial forms in the natural sciences he was wrong, so Leibniz thought, to believe that he could dispense with them in metaphysics. Without substantial forms or something like them, there would be no basis for treating material things as substances in a strict sense, for there would be no reason to regard a parcel of matter as a true unity (see *Supp.* 7) and, without a principle of identity, 'no body would ever last more than a moment' (*Discourse* §12).

Leibniz's defence of substantial forms was, however, more limited and his critique of mechanism more radical than what we have so far indicated. For, although he supposed in the *Discourse* that bodies are substances, he was soon to see that he could not hold both that substances are true unities, and therefore indivisible, and that bodies were substances in the strict sense (see *Supp.* 20). The substance of material things was, he concluded, derivative. A block of marble, for instance, was not a substance, strictly speaking, because it could be divided into two blocks. What made it substantial was that any parcel of matter was full of indivisible and immaterial substances — what Leibniz was later to term 'monads'.[16]

Leibniz's apparent defence of 'substantial forms' is therefore a use by him of an established terminology in order to defend a position more peculiarly his own. In rejecting substantial forms the mechanistic philosophers had removed an obstacle to developing a new physics, since such a physics needed to cut across the Aristotelian division of nature into essentially different kinds. But, in doing so, they were in danger also of rejecting something correct about the insistence on substantial forms — not only the requirement that substances, properly speaking, should have a principle of unity and identity but also the need, at bottom, to underpin the physical world with 'incorporeal natures' (see *Discourse* §10). Leibniz was thoroughly modern in accepting the importance of mechanistic explanations of nature. But he wished to resist the implications of a simple projection of such explanations into metaphysics, which he took to be materialism, determinism and a denial of any purpose in the world.

2.3 Modern philosophy and its religious implications

We have suggested that the persistence of Scholasticism in the seventeenth century in spite of the criticisms that were increasingly directed against it was due in large measure to the fact that it appeared to provide the philosophical framework most hospitable to orthodox Christianity. This accommodation between what was taken to be the thought of Aristotle and the teachings of the Bible was not achieved without difficulty nor, for that matter, without distortion of Aristotle. Nonetheless an accommodation was achieved that found its best expression in Thomas Aquinas's *Summa Theologica* (1259–64). Doubts about Aristotle — for instance as to whether his view of substantial forms was even consistent with belief in individual immortality — were provoked by scholars like *Averroes, but such doubts might be calmed by assuming that the substantial forms of human beings were souls in a Platonic sense. Leibniz is following in this tradition of adapting Aristotle's terminology to Christian purposes when he insists, in *Discourse* §12, that substantial forms are principles of identity in virtue of which an individual can be said to be the same at different times. In the case of human beings substantial forms are not just 'incorporeal natures' but immortal souls.

Another respect in which Aristotle had been adapted to the needs of Christian teaching relates to the doctrine of providence. Aristotle taught nothing about a providence, although he believed in a first cause of the universe. But Aristotelian science made extensive use of what he called '*final causes', and in this respect harmonised well with the Christian idea that the world is made with a purpose.

When Descartes and other moderns insisted that final causes should not be invoked in natural science and that all explanation in physics should be in terms of *efficient causes, they raised the bogies of mechanism, materialism and determinism. The Cartesians, following Descartes himself, had claimed that animals were machines — physical systems whose workings were to be understood in non-purposive terms — and others seemed, explicitly or implicitly, to extend the analogy in the obvious direction of human beings. A major aim of the *Discourse* was to provide a corrective to such tendencies, as is clear enough from a comparison of its contents with the unpublished piece we entitle 'Two sects of naturalists' (*Supp.* 9).

It required little reflection to detect such tendencies in Hobbes and Spinoza, who came to be dismissed with horror and without discussion in the late seventeenth century. Leibniz, who had a considerable respect for both of them, found himself on the defensive for as little as introducing Spinoza's name into correspondence.[17] There is no doubt that Leibniz shared the widespread concern at the materialistic and deterministic tendencies of the mechanical philosophy, but the philosopher against whom Leibniz's criticisms were above all directed was Descartes — partly, perhaps, because these tendencies were less obvious in his writings and partly because Descartes had come to be seen as the foremost representative of Modern philosophy.

René Descartes (1596–1650) was a French mathematician and

scientist of great distinction whose philosophy was seen by some as superseding all previous philosophy. His disciples — the *Cartesians — were often accused, by Leibniz (*Discourse* §17) amongst others, of adhering to his doctrines in as servile a way as the Scholastics adhered to what they took to be the doctrines of Aristotle. Descartes himself, by the radical distinction he drew between mind and body and by his arguments for the existence of a God, believed his philosophy to be entirely in harmony with orthodox Christianity. Religion and natural science were to be kept quite separate and the links between them made through metaphysics. Thus, while denying any place to purposes in the natural world with which the scientist was concerned, Descartes did not deny a providence. On the contrary, it seemed to many, Descartes provided a philosophy that gave an even more prominent place to God than did Aristotle's philosophy. In Aristotle, after all, the natural world only needed a 'prime mover' to bring it into being. Once in being, everything that happened was to be explained in terms of the essential natures of the substances into which the world was divided. Descartes's laws of motion (discussion in *Discourse* §17) required that the total quantity of motion in the universe was conserved. Without a conserver the train of events would quickly come to an end. The God of Descartes thus played a crucial continuing role in the universe.

A notorious and immediately recognised problem at the heart of Descartes's philosophy resulted from his separation of mind and body. Descartes supposed that in action and perception the two substances interacted. But it was unclear how, on his own terms, this was possible. The body, being an extended thing, could only affect or be affected by something with which it was spatially adjacent. That was a requirement of the *mechanical philosophy. But the mind, according to Descartes, was essentially different; essentially a thinking and not an extended substance. It follows from this that the mind is not spatially adjacent to anything else and so cannot affect or be affected by bodily substance.

Some of the *Cartesians quickly modified this part of Descartes's philosophy in a way that gave God an even more central role. They grasped the nettle of this difficulty and denied that there were those casual interactions whose existence Descartes had felt obliged to acknowledge. What they claimed was that when, for instance, someone intentionally raises an arm, the mental event is no more than an *occasional cause of the bodily event, i.e. occasions on which God intervenes to produce such an event. These 'communications' (to use Leibniz's phrase) between mind and body were not due to any real *influence, as the Scholastics had supposed. On the contrary, according to those who became known as 'occasionalists', the only true cause is God.

With such consequences it is not surprising that many religious philosophers, such as the priest Nicolas Malebranche (1638–1715), should find the Cartesian philosophical framework one they could readily accept. And, indeed, Leibniz himself had at one time claimed that the mechanical philosophy, because of its need for a conserver of the universe, offered the only plank against 'the shipwreck of atheism'.[18] Even in the 1680s, he was inclined to favour occasionalism as the only way of explaining how minds and bodies could 'communicate' with one another.[19]

Leibniz had long believed, however, that minds are genuine causes — a belief in which he followed Plato (see *Discourse* §20). This belief seemed to him to be compromised by occasionalism and thus to pose a problem for him whose solution, as is apparent from the beginning of *Discourse* §8 and elsewhere, is central to the 'system' first articulated in the *Discourse* (see Section 3 below). For Leibniz, the denial of real causal powers to creatures was, moreover, effectively a denial of their individuality.[20] This in turn was too close for comfort to denying that there were any substances other than God. In short, Malebranche's philosophy was too close to pantheism and *Spinozism.

In spite of these hazards, Leibniz was happy to represent his own philosophy as a development[21] from that of Malebranche. He was attracted by Malebranche's Platonism, including the thought that God created the most perfect and therefore most orderly universe — a thought that is prominent throughout the *Discourse* and on whose implications Leibniz dwells in its earlier sections. These implications were ones Malebranche had not considered sufficiently, Leibniz thought, or else he would have seen that he could not consistently suppose that God would create a universe which would require His constant intervention as a *deus ex machina*, as a producer of perpetual miracles.

Leibniz followed Malebranche in thinking that there were laws of grace as well as laws of nature, that God not only made a universe that was, miracles excepted, utterly orderly, but also observed an utter orderliness in His own decrees, including those that required the performance of miracles. Leibniz thus maintained that there was a general *order — what might be called a moral order — that in some way subsumed[22] the natural order ordained by God. We can understand what belongs to the natural order, but cannot fully understand the moral order. Miracles are those occurrences in the universe that are to us inexplicable (see *Discourse* §7). They are not an interruption by God of the general order but part of a pre-established harmony between things ordained by God at the creation of the universe.

The thought that God *observes* laws of grace makes those into eternal truths independent of the will of God and is one point at which Leibniz and Descartes were radically opposed. Descartes was so anxious to assert God's sovereignity that he even allowed that the truths of mathematics were created by God's will. Leibniz — here again following Plato — believed not only that the truths of mathematics (and logic) were eternal truths, but also that there were eternal truths of goodness, beauty and justice (*Discourse* §2). If, Leibniz contended, the world was good because God made it, what basis would there be for praising Him? Descartes's God was not the Christian God but an arbitrary despot. Leibniz, on the contrary, thought that a Christian philosophy would need to allow both that there are objective standards of perfection, independent of God's will, and that it is possible for us to know whether or not the world conforms to them. It must, in short, be possible to see Nature as the handiwork of a perfect God.

An immediate consequence of this view is that the perfection of God's world must be something of which natural science can give evidence. For Leibniz this evidence in turn was partly to be found in the fact that final causes are useful in the natural sciences, as he argues in *Discourse* §§19–22 (see also *Supp.* 10). Descartes was misguided in excluding final causes from the natural sciences. Worse still, such views could have dangerous consequences for religion by encouraging the thought that there were no purposes in the universe at all — an extension of Cartesianism, as it seemed to Leibniz, that was made by Spinoza (see *Supp.* 9).

Leibniz's defence of 'final causes, incorporeal natures and an Intelligent Cause' is, he writes, both 'to purge the mechanical philosophy of the profanity imputed to it' and 'to raise the minds of our philosophers from mere material considerations to more noble meditations' (*Discourse* §23). But it should not be supposed from these remarks that Leibniz regarded Aristotelianism as particularly conducive to 'noble meditations'. He pays tribute to the soundness of Aquinas (*Discourse* §11). But Leibniz compared Aristotle unfavourably with Plato, as being neither as deep (*Discourse* §27) nor as well confirmed by 'Holy Scripture and the Fathers' (*Discourse* §28). It is to Plato that Leibniz turned as the bulwark against materialism (*Discourse* §20).

2.4   Platonism and its problems

The *Discourse* is, as we have already seen, in many respects a defence of Plato. He is 'deeper' than Aristotle (*Discourse* §27) and more favoured by 'Holy Scripture and the Fathers' (*Discourse* §28). In contrast with some of the Modern philosophers, Plato showed a proper sense that an intelligent being was the cause of all things and hence that the world should ultimately be understood in terms of *final causes (*Discourse* §19). The world is accordingly to be understood, so Leibniz claimed, as the product of 'divine wisdom' (*Discourse* §6) and therefore as wholly harmonious and orderly. Human beings in turn are not to be understood as merely material beings whose knowledge is entirely dependent on the senses but, on the contrary, as minds that contain within themselves the capacity for knowing truths that they possess, in some sense, innately (*Discourse* §26).

Apart from the explicit references to Plato in the *Discourse* there are many other points at which Leibniz is defending Platonic or Neo-platonic doctrines. [23] This is particularly so in references to the soul. The stress on the unity, simplicity and, therefore, indestructibility of the soul is one that is to be found among Plato's arguments for immortality in the *Phaedo*. Other doctrines of a Neo-platonic origin are also to be found in the *Discourse* — for instance that each substance is a mirror of God and the universe (*Discourse* §9), *expressing it in its own way (§14), that it is a world to itself (§9 and §14) and that because it represents everything else in microcosm it is of infinite *extent. Such Neo-platonic ideas, though they may seem strange to us, would have been familiar to many of Leibniz's educated contemporaries. In treating them as paradoxical, however, Leibniz was acknowledging their initial implausibility. In an earlier work, he is highly critical of the Neo-platonists for debasing Plato's teachings and concludes with the remark that 'I know of no philosopher who had more correct opinions about incorporeal substances than Plato' (G vii 149).

But, if Plato was in this and in many other respects the philosopher whom Leibniz most revered, he took it for granted that Plato needed to be modified. For instance, he assumed that Plato's theory of forms or 'ideas' was, in its original form, unacceptable because these forms or 'ideas' were eternal beings existing independently of God. On the other hand, Leibniz was receptive to the Christian Platonist version of this theory according to which such 'ideas' exist independently of us but in the mind of God. Moreover, as we have seen, Leibniz wanted to insist that there are eternal truths (about justice, goodness, and so on) that are true independently of the will of God (see *Discourse* §2).

So here, as in many matters (see, for example, §26), Leibniz thought that Plato came closer to the truth than was generally supposed and that many of his doctrines, purged of certain errors and rightly interpreted, were still acceptable. He once remarked in correspondence: 'If someone were to reduce Plato to a system, he would render a great service to mankind, and it would then be clear that my own views approach his somewhat' (PPL 659, G iii 637). When the complaint was made of Augustine that his system 'was infected with Platonic language and opinions', Leibniz's rejoinder was that 'it is enriched and set off thereby' (*Supp.* 12).

Platonism was by no means out of fashion in the late seventeenth century, but it was regarded with considerable suspicion by orthodox theologians and seemed to many to be out of tune with Modern philosophy. [24] Leibniz acknowledged that this suspicion needed to be allayed in some measure by distancing himself from some contemporary forms of Platonism. His attack on the *quietists — 'false mystics, who deny individuality and action to the mind of the blessed' (PPL 594, Dutens II 224) — was not only an attack on certain of the Cartesians and Aristotelians but also on some of the Platonists as well. But the attack is in no way an acknowledgement of any fault in Plato, for Leibniz went on, 'I observe nothing in Plato that would lead me to conclude that minds do not conserve their own substance' (PPL 595, Dutens II 224). Platonism, in other words, can be made entirely consistent with the view of individual immortality that is required by Christian belief.

Leibniz indeed is not content merely to argue for the consistency of his Platonism with Christianity but that his principles are useful (§32) in promoting true piety and religion. He admits the necessity of the Christian revelation. But this, as summarised in §37, corroborates rather than supplements the view of human beings and their place in the universe that Leibniz claims to have substantiated.

Leibniz was not unusual in regarding Plato as a bastion against materialism.[25] But many of the Platonists over-reacted, in Leibniz's judgement, to the extent of denying the reality of matter entirely and therefore denying that there are any efficient causes in nature. Against those who invoked 'the *concurrence of God, or some soul or *Arché' (§10) to explain particular phenomena, Leibniz makes the same objection as he does to those who invoke *substantial forms. To do so is to mistake levels of explanation. At one level, for instance, it is indeed true that God is the cause of everything. But this is not to say that God should be mentioned in every explanation. It is, on the contrary, usually sufficient to explain things in terms of their efficient or what was sometimes called 'secondary' causes, in accordance with the known laws of nature. These laws are *subaltern or subordinate laws (§7 and §17) that follow from the laws of grace. But, since we do not know *how* they follow, our understanding of the world is limited in such a way that the laws of nature appear to us as an independent realm. It is as if nature has 'an empire within an empire' (*Supp*. 14) in which the material world appears to be governed by its own laws.And corresponding to this double kingdom are the twin sciences of physics and metaphysics.

Metaphysics can direct the enquiries of natural scientists by drawing attention to general principles, and Leibniz is anxious to insist on the 'utility' of a final causes perspective in physics (§19). But the double kingdom theory allows physics to be an autonomous science. An emphasis on final causes in a deeper understanding of the world need not, or so Leibniz thought, detract from the existence of efficient causes or from the importance of enquiring into them.

Physics and metaphysics are thus complementary sciences and a false view of the world results if notions proper to one are imported into the other. The notion of substantial forms belongs exclusively to metaphysics and has no place in the natural sciences (§10–11); whereas mechanistic explanations belong exclusively in the natural sciences and have no place in metaphysics. By his double kingdom theory, Leibniz sought both to condemn the naturalist philosophers (§9) as superficial and to distance himself from those Aristotelians and Platonists whose theories were out of tune with Modern philosophy.

At the time of writing the *Discourse*, Leibniz was unwilling to endorse the view of the Platonists that material bodies are not, strictly speaking, substances at all (§12 and 33). It is possible that he then believed that to deny that material bodies were substances would effectively be to deny the reality of matter. But, on his own principles, if there are efficient causes in nature then there must be substances to which they can be referred. In opposing the 'spiritualising' Platonists who denied efficient causes Leibniz seems to have been committed to insisting that there are material substances in some sense. Leibniz was aware that if substances are true unities and therefore indivisible, there was a difficulty about allowing that material bodies were substances in a strict sense. He later found, or believed he had found, a way of allowing that material bodies were substances only in a derivative sense and of finding a middle way between idealism and materialism. But, in the *Discourse*, he did not foresee this possible way out and settled instead for assuming that material bodies were substances in a strict sense.

If the *Discourse* is in part of a defence of Platonism it is nonetheless a work of Modern philosophy. It has a central problem, or at least a central cluster of problems, that was peculiarly Modern. Indeed, one way in which Platonism is defended in the *Discourse* is by being the inspiration for Leibniz's ingenious solution to these problems.

3 The central problem of the *Discourse*

When Leibniz had completed the *Discourse*, he wrote to Hesse-Rheinfels indicating that he had found 'new openings towards clarifying very great difficulties' (*Supp.* 1). But some of the questions he claimed to have dealt with — for instance the origin of evil — are dealt with only marginally. And in listing the others, Leibniz seems to have been catering to Hesse-Rheinfels' interest in religious and theological questions rather than offering an accurate summary of the main points of the *Discourse*. He did not mention the central problem of the *Discourse* — the problem whose solution he advertised later as constituting the heart of his 'system'. This is the problem he advertised by the title 'New System of the Nature and Communication of Substances' when he published his thoughts in an abridged and amended form in 1695.

We have already noted the centrality of the question about the nature of substances to Leibniz's metaphysical agenda. As against the *Cartesians, he insisted on a substance having a principle of unity and identity and for this reason thought there was something right after all about the doctrine of *substantial forms. As against Malebranche and the *occasionalists, Leibniz insisted that a substance must be capable of 'action', i.e., of initiating change and that, therefore, if there are to be created substances rather than one single substance as in Spinoza's philosophy, God cannot be held to be the only true cause.

The problem of the nature of created substances is, however, not only a problem about the relation between them and their Creator, but a problem about how they relate to one another. This problem, which Leibniz states abstractly as the problem of how substances can 'communicate' with one another, in turn subsumes problems that other philosophical agendas tend to state separately as the problem of perception and the mind-body problem, as well as the problem as to how one material body can 'communicate' with another. Leibniz himself deals with them separately in the *Discourse* (§14–15 and §33 respectively) though it is clear that he did not regard them as separable. It is in virtue of his solution to this problem, or cluster of problems, that Leibniz was to claim to be the author of a new system.

The problem is a complex one and in presenting it in a simplified form we plead the excuse that this was how Leibniz himself tended to present it. One source of the problem is the rejection by most Modern philosophers of Scholastic theories of interaction. Suárez had proposed, for instance, that this involved some kind of inflowing (*influx*) of one substance into another. But the postulation of such *influences was dismissed by Leibniz and others as a typically Scholastic piece of obscurantism. The Scholastic theory of perception involved the picture of a messenger *species that was transmitted by a material object when we see it. Malebranche subjected this view to a scathing attack in his *Search after Truth* (Book III, Part II, Ch. 2) pointing out, *inter alia*, that material objects could hardly be supposed to be continually giving off such species if they lost nothing in the process.

In 1679 Leibniz wrote to Malebranche agreeing with him that 'strictly speaking, bodies do not act on us' (PPL 201, G i 330). In a previous letter in 1679, he agreed with Malebranche on one reason for this, namely, that it is impossible to conceive how a substance that is extended but lacks thought can act on a substance that is unextended and 'has nothing but thought' (PPL 709, G i 327). He therefore agreed with the *occasionalists in denying that bodies can act on minds and that, on Descartes's own terms, the interaction he supposed between mind and body was possible.

Leibniz thought in any case that if matter was conceived in Cartesian terms as explicable wholly in terms of its geometrical properties it was impossible for material bodies to be substances in a full sense since Cartesian matter can only transmit motion imparted to it and cannot initiate change. For this reason, Leibniz had been inclined to believe that minds were the only substances. But even this view was threatened by the arguments of Malebranche and the occasionalists. They raised the bogey Leibniz is anxious to lay in the *Discourse* of a world in which no creature has true causal powers and where only God has the power to initiate change — a Spinozistic world in which there are no substances other than God.

Leibniz took some time, however, to realise that occasionsalism raised the bogeys of Spinozism and quietism. He was, at least for a time, himself an occasionalist, even endorsing a view of perception close to that of Malebranche. Malebranche had offered his account of perception — summarised in his doctrine that we see all things in God — as a hypothesis, as proved by being the only remotely plausible explanation. Malebranche adopted a procedure that Leibniz himself was impressed by and later followed himself, namely, a method of exclusion. If a hypothesis is a possible one and all the other possible explanations are seriously faulty to the point where they can be ruled out, this Malebranche took to constitute a 'proof' (though not a 'demonstration') of the hypothesis.[27]

Leibniz at one stage thought that the hypothesis that we see all things in God was acceptable on this basis:

> God is the sole immediate object of the mind, outside of itself ... it is
> only through the medium of God our ideas represent to us what passes
> in the world; for *on no other supposition can it be conceived* how the
> body can act on the soul, or how different created substances can
> communicate with one another ... (*System of Theology*, p. 73, italics
> added).

This is not quite Malebranche's position since, although Leibniz
agreed that ideas are in God, he seems always to have held the
view of the *Discourse* (§28) that there must also be ideas in us.
What he seems to have supposed in the *System of Theology*,
however, was that all action of one created substance on another
was mediated by God. He seems indeed to have held the very
*deus ex machina view of God's role in the world that he
complains of in the *Discourse* and later writings as involving
perpetual miracles (see *Supp.* 5). When he criticises Malebranche for
such views — inaccurately, as has frequently been pointed out[28] —
he seems to be criticising a view he had formerly held himself.

However that may be, Leibniz continued to agree with the
occasionalists that our experiences are not produced in us by
material objects. But he was no longer willing to invoke the
continual intervention of God. Perception happens naturally, so an
explanation in terms of miracles should, Leibniz thought, be ruled
out. By such a process of exclusion Leibniz was 'insensibly' led to
toy with a hypothesis that was inspired by the Neo-platonist ideas
referred to in the previous section — what he described to Foucher
as 'a pleasing opinion' (see *Supp.* 18). The hypothesis involved the
extraordinary thought that everything that happens to a substance
somehow arises spontaneously from within itself.

In the *New System*, in which Leibniz acknowledged his debt to
Malebranche for showing what cannot take place, he narrates the
emergence of this hypothesis in these terms:

> Being constrained, then, to admit that it is impossible for the soul or
> any other created substance to receive something from without, except
> by the divine omnipotence, I was led insensibly to an opinion which
> surprised me, but which seems inevitable, and which has, in fact, very
> great advantages and very significant beauties. This is that we must say
> that God has originally created the soul, and every other real unity, in
> such a way that everything must arise from its own nature by a perfect
> *conformity* to things without.
> (PPL 457, G iv 484)

It is this opinion that is developed in Neo-platonic terms in §§9 and 14–15 of the *Discourse*. Each substance is a world apart, not acted on by any other substance. But it is a microcosm of the universe as a whole so that in some sense the whole universe is represented in it or, in the language of the *Discourse*, *expressed by it. As the universe itself is a mirror of God, so each substance is a *mirror and indeed strives to imitate God (§9). But each individual substance is unique, for it expresses the universe in a slightly different way from any other substance. It is because of a correspondence between the *appearances of each individual substance that causal relationships exist in nature. In *Discourse* §14, Leibniz attempts to explain why one thing is said to be the cause and a concomitant thing its effect by suggesting that what is called the 'cause' is more perfect in its expression — more clear and distinct — and the other more confused. But, strictly speaking, each substance produces its phenomena spontaneously, from itself, and is not acted on by any other created substance.

Many (to Leibniz) agreeable consequences follow from this hypothesis — not least that since substances cannot be acted on by other substances, they are naturally indestructible (§9). But the hypothesis itself was too *paradoxical to be presented as a plausible solution to the problem of the communication of substances without further argument in its favour. Leibniz accordingly sought higher ground by arguing that the hypothesis was derivable from principles that everyone ought to accept and were indeed commonly accepted. The *Discourse* begins by stating and developing the implications of these principles and it is from them that the work derives its systematic character.

4 The structure and method of the *Discourse*

The *Discourse* may be divided into three main parts. In the first part (§1–16), Leibniz states and gives preliminary development to his two leading principles. These are: (1) that God has chosen to create the most perfect world, i.e. the one which combines the greatest possible order with the greatest possible variety; (2) it is in the nature of an individual substance to have a concept so complete that from it can be derived everything that is true of that substance. These principles are combined to produce some of the more remarkable claims of the work — for instance, that everything in the universe is connected with everything else and that no two individual substances are exactly alike. From these in turn Leibniz infers that each individual substance is a mirror of the entire universe, reflecting it from a distinctive point of view.

The second part of the *Discourse* (§§17–22) is concerned with natural science. Leibniz attacks two central features of Cartesian physics: (a) the laws of motion and (b) the exclusion of final causes from physics. Leibniz puts forward his own proposal that it is the total quantity of force that is conserved and not the total quantity of motion (§17). From this he infers that the *Cartesian demand that nature is to be explained in terms of the geometric properties of matter alone is erroneous, and that the general principles of corporeal nature are metaphysical (§18). This leads him to a defence of final causes in physics, one that links with his first leading principle about nature being ultimately governed by divine wisdom (§19). Having thus disposed of a purely materialist view of nature, Leibniz quotes Plato in his support (§20). He then goes on to explain how he sees final cause (purposive) and efficient cause (mechanistic) explanations as complementary rather than mutually exclusive (§21–2).

The third part of the *Discourse* is concerned with spirits and their relation to God. Sections §23–9 deal with topics arising from the Malebranche-Arnauld controversy and overlap in content (though with differences of detail) with Leibniz's 1684 paper 'Meditations on Knowledge, Truth and Ideas' (*Supp*. 11). From a largely epistemological discussion Leibniz turns to one that is largely theological (§30–1), in which he addresses questions about Grace, the origin of evil and the cause of sin. Finally, he argues for the utility of his principles (in particular, his two leading principles) in matters of piety and religion. The system of the *Discourse* offers a good account, it is claimed, of the relation of the soul to the body, of immortality, of the special excellence of spirits, of their freedom and of their independence from everything except God Himself. The perfection of the world is not just a metaphysical but a moral one. Leibniz concludes by showing how what he says fits in with central tenets of orthodox Christianity.

In his 'grande lettre' to Foucher of 1686 (*Supp*. 18), Leibniz does not explain how his system is to be derived from principles. Instead, he claims that his method is that of the geometers, of supposing certain axioms and attempting to derive from them as much as can be demonstrated with full rigour. The axioms may themselves stand in need of further demonstration, but we need not — indeed should not — await this demonstration of them. For we can in the meantime use these demonstrations in order to put an end to disputes. Leibniz's thought seems to have been that his starting-points themselves would receive confirmation by proving to be fruitful in solving problems, that is by setting matters in such a clear light that the difficulties will be resolved and the disputes brought to an end. It seems to be in this spirit that the remarks, in *Discourse* §33: 'I believe that persons able to meditate will see advantage in our principles in just this, that it is easy to see just in what the connection is between soul and body, apparently inexplicable by any other means.' It seems that these principles must be the two leading principles mentioned in the previous section — 'the grand principle of the perfection of the operations of God and the notion of the substance including all the events with all their circumstances' (§32). The first of these principles is the one introduced in §1–7. The second is introduced in §8 and is followed in §9–15 by discussions of their implications.

In fact, Leibniz was not content to put forward his principle that the complete notion of every individual substance includes everything that is true of it as a basic supposition. In *Discourse* §8 he claims that it follows from a view of the nature of the proposition that he attributes to Aristotle, namely that in every true proposition the notion of the predicate is contained in that of the subject — the principle of *inesse*.[29]

Leibniz's method combines both *a priori* and *a posteriori* strategies. Neither, he seems to have supposed, would be complete in itself. The *a posteriori* strategies are problem-centred and relate to the ability of a system to explain the phenomena or to solve problems. Leibniz sometimes suggested (e.g. in *Discourse* §33) that persons capable of meditation would be convinced of his principles because of their explanatory success. But he did not regard the principles as mere suppositions. They were commonly accepted[30] principles which could be accepted on good authority.

The *a priori* strategies begin with these principles and would convince those who accepted them of whatever could strictly be demonstrated from them. The *a priori* strategies also provide ways of connecting different parts of the system with one another. The *Discourse* develops these less rigorously than 'Primary Truths'

(*Supp.* 19). But nowhere did Leibniz attempt the kind of rigorous demonstration that he held up as called for in metaphysics. This may be because he had difficulty in finding suitable principles — ones that would command universal assent and from which many conclusions could be drawn — with which to begin.

In practice, Leibniz relied more on *a posteriori* strategies to defend his system than on *a priori* ones. His *New System* was largely defended as a hypothesis and, indeed, it was only when Foucher claimed it was no more than a hypothesis that Leibniz was to insist that, on the contrary, it all followed from his view of substances as true unities (G iv 494). The *New System* does not depend on either of the principles Leibniz took as his starting points in the *Discourse*. This may be because it is less comprehensive or because Leibniz did not expect to persuade Cartesians by invoking them. The *inesse* principle largely disappears from view in Leibniz's later writings and its place is taken by the principle of sufficient reason — a principle that in 1686 was put forward only as a corollary. [31] (See *Supp.* 19, para. 4).

The *Discourse on Metaphysics* is neither a final nor a complete statement of Leibniz's metaphysics. But in some ways, it is the most comprehensive, the clearest and best organised. Where some works give prominence to his *a priori* strategies (e.g. *Supp.* 19) and others, like the *New System*, exaggerate his *a posteriori* strategies and so give a distorted impression of Leibniz's method, the *Discourse* makes use of both strategies as integral to his method and as complementary to one another.

Leibniz would undoubtedly have liked to produce a definitive metaphysics. But even if the hope of such finality was not utopian, it was hardly one that could be nurtured at a time when there was little that the various philosophical sects could find in common. Leibniz's philosophy was far removed from the confident modernism of Descartes or even Spinoza. What were certainties for Descartes were reduced to articles of faith for the Cartesians, with their critics gibing that you needed to be a Cartesian to find 'clear and distinct' what they alleged to be so.[32] Perhaps only a provisional metaphysics could have been ventured in the circumstances. At all events, Leibniz's metaphysics was never more than that. The provisional character of the *Discourse* as a statement of Leibniz's metaphysics may, in this perspective, be seen not as a defect but as a positive virtue.

5 Achievement and problems

The *Discourse* is, in spite of its shortness, an extremely ambitious work. It purports to resolve a number of scientific, theological and metaphysical problems in ways that its readers would not find too contentious. It provides a perspective that acknowledges some of the cherished insights of very disparate groups of thinkers and which, or so Leibniz hoped, Scholastic Aristotelians, Cartesians, Platonists and others might all be persuaded to share. More specifically, it is critical of both Malebranche and Arnauld, but in such a way that each might see in Leibniz's system a resolution of their differences.

The philosophy of the *Discourse* is inseparable from its scientific and theological content. It is not only an attempt to bridge the schisms between the different philosophical parties — itself a huge task — but to provide a basis on which all thinking people might agree. Leibniz's system is intended to provide a safeguard against the threat of materialism and atheism. Indeed it is, or was intended to be taken as, a Christian philosophy, as the basis for a consensus about essentials that would allow the Christian denominations to live in harmony with one another. It would be hard not to be impressed by the grandeur of Leibniz's project, and indeed it is as much by virtue of his encyclopaedic vision as by virtue of his specific doctrines that Leibniz came to enjoy his posthumous status as the first in a line of great German philosophers. This is worth stressing, since Leibniz himself largely failed to achieve any of the objectives which the *Discourse*, had it been published, might have contributed to fulfilling. These objectives largely remained those he pursued in his later writings, though the Malebranche-Arnauld controversy, important though it was in the 1680s, naturally receded from his concerns.

Any critical appraisal of the *Discourse* would require a work many times its length. But a proper understanding of it is, we believe, enhanced by, and may indeed require, an appropriate critical distance from it. If we ask ourselves whether we find the work convincing we are likely to become quickly dissatisfied at the fact that it contains so many unargued assumptions that we would be inclined to question, for instance, whether the universe is basically made up of one kind of thing, namely substances, and that these substances are all fundamentally similar. Leibniz does indeed argue elsewhere for some of things he assumes in the *Discourse* (e.g. the existence of God, see *Supp.* 4). But any philosopher has to start from somewhere. And the merit, perhaps, of identifying the unargued assumptions of a work is that these may be assumptions shared by the author and his or her contemporaries.

A less distant approach is to consider how those for whom a work is written might have responded to it. It is not always easy to know for whom a work is written, but it is not too difficult in the case of the *Discourse*, nor indeed for most of Leibniz's writings. The *Discourse* is directed to certain constituencies of opinion and we can talk of *its* problems without imposing our perspective on it. Its problems lie in those areas where the various categories of reader he had in mind might reasonably have remained unconvinced and at those points where unresolved tensions remain in the account Leibniz gives. Since Leibniz presented versions of his system to which some of his contemporaries replied, it is not difficult to locate where some of these problems lie. Others are less obvious. In presenting some of these problems we make no pretence of being comprehensive and leave to interested readers the task of pursuing the question whether, and if so on what terms, Leibniz would have been able to solve them. We present them in order in which they appear in the *Discourse*:

(a) God's freedom

Leibniz, in common with orthodox Christians, wanted to uphold the view of God as a wholly perfect being who created the universe. He inferred from this that the universe must itself be the most perfect possible. Moreover, he wished to insist (§2) that the perfection of the universe is something we can judge from its orderliness and other features and that the standards of perfection themselves are independent of God's will. But if God is essentially perfect then He would have no choice but to create a world which complies absolutely with these independent standards of perfection. God, in short, has no free will. Indeed, although Leibniz keeps using the world 'will', it is not clear that there is any more room for talk of God's *will* in Leibniz's philosophy than Spinoza had allowed for in his. Leibniz's thought he could avoid Spinozism by claiming that this is only one of an infinite number of possible worlds. But he cannot, on his own terms, allow that there is more than one best possible world. For then there would not be sufficient reason for God to create *this* world rather than one of the other perfect ones. Leibniz is thus faced with a dilemma: either God is not free, in which case it is inappropriate to praise Him for His works; or else there is some arbitrariness about God's dealings with His creation, in which case the principle of sufficient reason is not completely without exception. Leibniz's voluntarist critics, like Arnauld, who insisted on the arbitrary and to us mysterious nature of God, would have preferred instead to allow that, *pace* Leibniz (§2), the universe is good because God made it and not the other way around.[33]

(b)   God's perfection and the perfection of the universe
It is essential to Leibniz's project of deriving his metaphysics at least partly from a view of God's perfections that we do have some knowledge of what it means to say that God is perfect. Leibniz's view involves projecting on to God, more or less self-consciously, an ideal of scientific theory and an ideal of natural order, namely that it requires the fewest hypotheses and permits the derivation of the richest variety of effects (§5). This projection is not, on Leibniz's own terms, objectionable. But he is caught at this point in a problem that compounds the previous one. If the world is perfect because God made it, then any attempt to talk of God's perfection in terms of our standards of perfection is anthropomorphic, a mere projection.[34] In order to bring the voluntarists round to his way of thinking, Leibniz would need to be able to argue that his ideal of a scientific theory was one that conformed to absolute standards of rationality expressible as eternal truths and not merely one that was confirmed by scientific practice in preferring certain theories (e.g. the Copernican, see §5) to others.

(c)   Miracles
A further related difficulty is that Leibniz's insistence on the absolutely law-governed character of the general order leads him to deny that there are any arbitrary interventions on God's part in the universe. He professes to retain 'miracles' (§7) but his claim that everything that is true of any given substance is contained in its full concept is expressly intended to include miracles (§16). He is therefore committed to holding that nothing that happens in the

universe is supernatural — what is distinctive about miracles is that
we cannot understand why they happen, according to Leibniz, not
that they are specially imposed on the ordinary course of events.

That Leibniz held there were no miracles in the ordinarily
accepted sense is evident from the criticism he sometimes made of
Malebranche that his *occasionalism required the appeal to a
perpetual miracle, to a *deus ex machina* (see, for instance, *Supp.*
5). This is, in a way, unfair to Malebranche, since Malebranche
expressly denied that there were miracles in the voluntarist sense
of arbitrary acts of divine intervention.[35] The issue between them
concerns only whether the laws of grace operate independently of
the individual substances, as Malebranche held, or whether they
operate through the natures of the substances themselves, as
Leibniz seems to have held (§16) and indeed must hold to sustain
the view that *everything* that happens to a substance arises
spontaneously from its own nature.

(d) Human freedom

Leibniz's principle that the complete concept of every individual
substance contains everything that is true of it is one he derives
from a principle held by the Scholastics and also used by
Arnauld.[36] This is the principle of *inesse*, namely, that in a true
proposition the concept of the predicate is contained in that of the
subject. This principle had usually been taken to apply only to
abstract or necessary truths and carried with it the thought that
such truths depended on the principle of contradiction. Leibniz
extends this principle to substances and therefore to truths that
were usually taken to be contingent.

In doing so, he immediately raised the worry that he was really
claiming that, at bottom, there were no contingent truths and that
(like Spinoza) he held that only human ignorance made it appear
that any truth was other than necessary. The problem of fatalism is
one Arnauld immediately suspected when he read Leibniz's
summaries and Leibniz himself was aware that he needed to
forestall just such an objection (§13). Leibniz has widely been
supposed to be a fatalist and because of this and the foregoing
problems, even a secret *Spinozist. And certainly he must, to
avoid the charge, find a way of allowing that the universe can be
fully described by truths that are reducible, upon analysis, to
tautologies without being obliged to admit that there are no

contingent truths. He thought he could. But that he could is not clear from the *Discourse* and is clear, if at all, only in the more careful explanations he offered to Arnauld or in other writings in the post-*Discourse* period.[37]

(e)   Material substances

Leibniz claimed in the *Discourse* to be offering an account of substance which was at least consistent with supposing that there are material substances in a strict sense. If this is so, then some substances are spatial and therefore space must be something real, as was commonly assumed. But, on Leibniz's own terms, space is a *continuum and a continuum is infinitely divisible. That being so, there must be something more to a material substance than extension and its modifications (§12). This something more is a *substantial form. But, as Arnauld pointd out[38] this account is fraught with difficulties. A block of marble, for instance, may be cut in two, yielding two blocks of marble. And this process can, at least to some extent, be repeated. What becomes of the indivisible substantial form by courtesy of which the original block of marble was a proper substance? Leibniz was obliged to admit that blocks of marble were not, strictly speaking, substances at all, but only aggregates. Eventually he arrived at the position of his 'monadology' — that the only true substances are non-spatial and non-material things although (except in the case of God) they were invariably associated in some way with matter. Matter and space are not real things, he came round to saying, but well-founded phenomena. Some of the later Leibniz's most interesting pieces of metaphysical reasoning are attempts to work out the details of this aspect of his philosophy.[39] They have no counterpart in the *Discourse* except in an unresolved problem.

(f)   The theory of expression

Leibniz's theory of expression is bound up with his predelictions for Neo-platonic views about the soul and the cosmos. Their plausibility depends on these views being made an integral part of a system that is able to convince by its solution to other problems (see Section 3 above). The thought that every substance is a microcosm of the universe as a whole, *expressing it from its own point of view, would not only have seemed implausible in itself, but Leibniz failed to make it clear or even coherent. Leibniz severely curtailed his discussion of expression in revising his first draft, removing some of the more specific claims. But he was tempted to say that when one substance was the (occasional) cause of some event in another, the first had ideas that were more clear and distinct and the other ideas that were more confused. It is difficult to see how this could possibly apply to substances other than minds if his later account (§24) of clear, distinct and confused ideas is correct. There is little doubt that Leibniz's reason for putting less emphasis on his theory of expression in his later writings was that he himself was not happy with it and did not expect others to find it convincing.[40]

(g) The alleged error in Descartes's laws of motion

The claim by Descartes and his followers that the material world could and should be explained entirely in terms of the geometrical properties of matter was one for which they were especially celebrated. It was easy to doubt whether their programme could actually be carried out and to assume that matter must have other properties than those the *Cartesians were prepared to admit. Leibniz had long been unhappy about the Cartesian programme but by 1686 he thought he could demonstrate an error in Descartes's reasoning that even the Cartesians would have admit (§17). He published his 'Brief Demonstration' in March of that year and it provoked a considerable controversy.[41] Neither it nor his subsequent work on dynamics proved to be the cutting edge against the Cartesian view of matter that he had hoped. The verdict of subsequent scientific theorising, as often in such controversies, was not so much to support one side against the other but to move on to a still different set of concepts.

(h) The mind-body problem

Leibniz followed Malebranche in making use of a method of exclusion in order to support his account of the communication of substances.[42] But the method is in many respects faulty, and is unconvincing to those who are immediately attracted by an explanation that is not considered. Foucher, in his reply to Leibniz's 'New System', distanced himself from any of the explanations Leibniz considered of the mind-body relation. Foucher was not happy with either occasionalism or Leibniz's pre-established harmony and was no defender of Scholastic

theories. At the same time, he did not accept either that one of
them must be right or that the relation of mind and body was (as
Leibniz put it in §33) inexplicable by any other means. Foucher
favoured an interactionist account, only with a different theory of
interaction (G iv 489f).

Leibniz, for his part, was too wedded to a view of substances as
simple, indestructible, self-contained entities to be able to favour
an interactionist theory. He later made it explicit that only
complex things could naturally interact, by the parts of one
affecting parts of the other.[43] Foucher expressed surprise that
Leibniz should embarrass himself with the difficulties of the
Cartesians (G iv 489). But Foucher ought not to have been
surprised. Leibniz, in spite of his willingness to criticise Descartes,
agreed with much of Descartes's account of the mind.[44] Doubtless
he would have insisted that Descartes himself showed an
unacknowledged debt to Plato and Augustine in his defence of a
simple and indestructible thinking substance. But Leibniz himself
was no more consistently able to embrace an interactionist account
of the mind-body relation than Descartes.[45]

These are no more than a sample of the difficulties left
unresolved by the *Discourse* and, indeed for the most part, by
Leibniz's later philosophy. His importance as a philosopher was
not due to any consensus that he had overcome them. Rather, as
we have already suggested, it is due to his encyclopaedic vision of
how the integration of the intellectual world might be achieved.
Such an integration was not, of course, universally desired. But
Leibniz's vision was taken up by Christian Wolff (1679–1754) and
in the eighteenth century the so-called Leibniz-Wolff philosophy
became an orthodoxy in German universities. That is not to say
that even Leibniz's limited number of published writings were
widely read, apart from his *Theodicy*. It is indeed only in the
twentieth century that the *Discourse on Metaphysics* acheived its
status as a classic of philosophy.

Notes

1 Aiton (1985) gives particular attention to Leibniz's work in mathematics and natural science and is helpful to the student of philosophy for the wider context it provides.

2 Nicolas Malebranche (1638–1715) and Antoine Arnauld (1612–1694) were both French philosophers of considerable importance in the period. Arnauld had been one of Descartes's critics but, like Malebranche, found much in Descartes's philosophy he could accept. For the connection between Leibniz and Malebranche, Robinet (1955), which collects together the primary materials, is indispensable. For an account of the background to Leibniz's *Discourse*, see Loemker (1947). Loemker translates at the end of this article some of Leibniz's notes on the Malebranche-Arnauld controversy.

3 Malebranche's *Treatise* was divided into 'discourses' and into numbered sections. Leibniz seems to have taken this work as his model for what was his first extended essay in French. Robinet (1955) draws attention to the overlap in contents that particulary affects the first seven sections of Leibniz's 'discours'.

4 See Aiton (1985, pp. 72–3 and elsewhere) for details of Leibniz's relations with Arnauld.

5 The main concession Leibniz gained from Arnauld related to Leibniz's principle of **inesse*, which Arnauld had initially thought committed Leibniz to fatalism. But though Leibniz made much of this concession, the *Discourse* goes further than Malebranche in theological directions Arnauld thought already too extreme in Malebranche, as we bring out further in Section 5. That the early sections of the *Discourse* contain a sometimes bitter attack on a conception of God which Arnauld himself was passionately committed to defending may be one reason why he was never sent the full text. At any rate Leibniz was well aware of the fact that Arnauld, in opposing Malebranche on the 'rule of the best', was also committed to resisting one of his own cardinal principles (see *Theodicy* §203).

6 Schmitt (1981) suggests that 'scholasticism generally lost its hold on the more progressive and up-to-date universities during the fifty years around 1700' (p. 179).

7   In the year before Leibniz wrote his *Discourse* Louis XIV had revoked the Edict of Nantes and stimulated a fresh wave of persecution of Protestants in France. Also in 1685 the Inquisition finally succeeded in trying and imprisoning the well-known *quietist Miguel de Molinos. Arnauld's position, as the leader of the Catholic *Jansenist sect, was far from secure and he was obliged to flee Paris for a time during Leibniz's 1686–90 correspondence with him. Leibniz's attempts at reconciliation between the Churches were pursued at a time when Catholic orthodoxy was becoming increasingly assertive. He may well have thought that his efforts were all the more necessary and have been part spurred into writing the *Discourse* because of the increasing intolerance. At all events he can hardly have taken the view that (with the benefit of hindsight) we cannot easily avoid, namely, that these efforts never had any prospect of being more than futile.

8   Malebranche's *Treatise* was put on the Catholic *Index of Prohibited Books* in 1689. His *Search after Truth* was not added till 1709. It is uncertain how much the readership of these books was affected by these actions.

9   Superficially indeed Leibniz seems to be much more of a Scholastic philosopher than he really was because of his willingness to clinch an argument with a Latin maxim such as *actiones sunt *suppositorum* or *praedicatum *inest subjecto*, both invoked in *Discourse* §8.

10   At least this was what Leibniz seems to have taken for granted. Brown (1984) argues that the appeal to authoritative opinion has a key place in Leibniz's methodology (pp. 70–1). This appears to be Leibniz's licence in the *Discourse* for his two major assumptions — his principle of the perfection of God's operations and his *inesse* principle.

11   Leibniz himself expressly acknowledged this. His articles for the Leipzig *Acta Eruditorum* were, he said, in the Scholastic style whereas when writing for other journals he adapted himself more to the style of the Cartesians (G iii 625).

12   Leibniz read Berkeley's *Principles of Human Knowledge* and wrote of it to a Scholastic Jesuit correspondent (Des Bosses) in highly dismissive terms. 'The Irishman who attacks the reality of bodies seems neither to offer suitable reasons nor to explain his position sufficiently. I suspect that he belongs to the class of men who want to be known for their paradoxes' (PPL 609, G ii 492). But privately Leibniz was more sympathetic to Berkeley, being content (in his remarks at the end of his own copy of the *Principles*) to suggest that Berkeley need not have expressed himself so paradoxically and that he could agree with much of what he had read. See Brown (1984, pp. 42–3).

13   In a preface to an edition of a work by Nizolius that Leibniz was called upon to prepare in 1670, he wrote? 'Nominalists are those who believe that all things except individual substances are mere names; they therefore deny the reality of abstract terms and universals forthright.' (PPL 128, G iv 157.)

14   This is perhaps the explanation for the vacillation between

'scholastics', 'new scholastics' and 'moderns' in the drafting of *Discourse* §3. The voluntaristic theology criticised in this section was a counterpart of nominalism.

15 See for instance, *Principles of Philosophy*, Part II.

16 Leibniz begins a later (1714) summary of his system — his *Principles of Nature and of Grace* — by distinguishing simple from compound substances: '*Substance* is a being capable of action. It is simple or compound. *Simple substance* is that which has no parts. Compound substance is a collection of simple substances, or *monads. Monas* is a Greek word signifying unity or that which is one ...' (PPL 636, G vi 598).

17 See, for instance, PPL 533, G ii 262.

18 In a letter written in 1669 and published by Leibniz in the following year (PPL 102, G i 26).

19 In his *System of Theology* (p. 73). See below Section 3.

20 This is a recurring theme in Leibniz's criticism of the *quietists — 'false mystics, who deny individuality and action to the mind of the blessed' (PPL 594, *Dutens* II 224). Those who maintain that only God acts virtually affirm that there is nothing apart from God. Criticising the world soul of the *Averroists, Leibniz remarks: 'Spinoza, who recognises only one single substance, is not far from the doctrine of a single universal spirit, and even the Neo-Cartesians, who hold that only God acts, affirm it, seemingly unaware' (PPL 554, G vi 530).

21 In a letter to l'Hôpital, who was in close touch with Malebranche, Leibniz suggested that Malebranche be urged to consider his system. He went on: 'It can perhaps be said that it is not so much a reversal as a development of his doctrine and that it is to him that I owe my foundations in this subject' (GM ii 299).

22 Hence Leibniz's use of the word *'subaltern' to describe laws of nature (§17). The thought is that the laws of nature should actually be derivable from the laws of grace. This is not to say that we can make the derivation, only that such connections would be an expected corollary of the perfect orderliness of the universe (§5).

23 See MacDonald Ross (1983, pp. 125–34) for a good discussion and further reading on this topic. Among the other Neo-platonic doctrines of the *Discourse* is Leibniz's account of creation as *emanation. More generally, Leibniz believed that the kind of harmony there was in the universe meant that there were many fundamental analogies, for instance between souls and other substances so that other substances can be understood as being analogous to the human soul, possessing something analogous to appetite and perception. (See, for instance, the 'New System', PPL 454, G iv 479).

24 Many of the heresies by which orthodox Christians believed their religion had been plagued have a Platonic origin. Renaissance Neo-platonism, moreover, served as a framework for integrating a number of magical, mystical and pseudo-scientific traditions (see *Schmitt*, pp. 230 and 193). That these were found dubious or even subversive seems clear from

the attentions of the Inquisition to Neo-platonists such as Giordano
Bruno (1548–1600) and Leibniz's friend, Franciscus Mercurius van Hel-
mont (1614–98).

25   So did the Cambridge Platonist Henry More (1614–87) and others
of the 'spiritualising authors' Leibniz discusses in his *New Essays* (p. 72).
The Platonic inspiration of Berkeley's idealism emerges explicitly in his
late work *Siris* and account for many of the striking points of affinity
between his philosophy and Leibniz's. See *Brown* (1984, *passim*) for some
of these affinities.

26   This is an authentically Leibnizian contrast. In a later writing
Leibniz claims: 'our view [of pre-established harmony] combines what is
good in the hypotheses of both Epicurus and Plato, of both the greatest
materialists and the greatest idealists ...' (PPL 578, G iv 560).

27   Malebranche offered a classification of 'all the ways external objects
can be seen' and went on to remark:

> We can know objects in only one of these ways. Let us examine,
> without prejudice, and without fear of the difficulty of the question,
> which is the likeliest way. Perhaps we can resolve the question with
> some clarity though we do not pretend to give *demonstrations that will
> seem incontrovertible to everyone;* rather we merely give *proofs that will
> seem very persuasive to those who consider them carefully*, for one
> would appear presumptuous were one to speak otherwise.
> (*Search after Truth*, p. 219, italics added).

Leibniz, in his French writings, seems to echo Malebranche's strategy
when presenting his own rival account of the communication of substances and the mind-body problem. He wrote to Bossuet, for instance:

> I hope that this great problem will be resolved in such a clear manner,
> that that of itself will serve as a proof to judge that we have found the
> key to some of these things ...
> (*Correspondance de Bossuet*, Vol. 6, pp. 527 f).

That his is the only likely explanation is a point made by Leibniz in
Discourse §33.

28   See the discussion under 'Miracles' in Section 5.

29   The exact argument of §8 has been a matter on which commentators have disagreed. See Broad (1949) and Nason (1942).

30   Leibniz begins the *Discourse* by appealing to the 'most commonly
accepted' notion of God (§1) as the basis of what he then goes on to argue.
His other principle is one that is 'acknowledged' (§8).

31   See Brown (1984, pp. 111–12 and 119–20) for a further discussion
of this point.

32   For an example of Leibniz's own use of this gibe see PPL 293, G iv
425.

33   Spinoza (*Ethics*, I, Prop. XXXIII, Note II) offered a penetrating
critique of the position Leibniz took in the controversy. Spinoza claims

that there is more truth in what was later called the 'voluntarist' view, i.e. 'the theory which subjects all things to the will of an indifferent deity, and asserts that they are all dependent on his *fiat*'.

34 See Notes on *Discourse* below, note 3.

35 For instance, in his *Dialogues on Metaphysics and on Religion* (1688) Malebranche writes: '... God never performs miracles; He never acts according to particular volitions against His own laws, for the order does not demand or permit it' (Malebranche, 1688, ed. Ginsberg, 1923, p. 129). Malebranche unfortunately, refused to be drawn into discussion with Leibniz about the respective merits of their two metaphysical systems.

36 See *The Art of Thinking*, Part IV, ch. 6. Arnauld used this principle as a test of axioms in place of Descartes's criterion of 'clearness and distinctness' and Leibniz seems (*Supp.* 11) to have supported this use of it, though he usually ascribes the principle to Aristotle on the basis of its use by the Scholastic Aristotelians.

37 For an account of how Leibniz might avoid the charge of fatalism, see Brown (1984, 9.1–9.2). The most important letter in this part of the correspondence is the long letter Leibniz sent to Arnauld on 14 July 1686. See Parkinson (1970) for an account of Leibniz's changing views on freedom of the will.

38 In his letter of 28 September 1686.

39 See, for instance, Leibniz's correspondence with Samuel Clarke.

40 This is not to say that Leibniz did not continue to believe that something like the theory of expression must be right. In the 'New System', for instance, he alludes to the representative character of each substance and even remarks in parenthesis that substances express the universe. But he did not elaborate and indeed left out from his draft a passage in which he had elaborated a little (G iv 475).

41 See Costabel, (1960) and Papineau (1977). Leibniz's dynamics were given greater prominence in his later presentations of his system, particularly in the 1690s.

As it would have required a lengthy explanation, quite out of proportion to its importance in the *Discourse*, we have not sought to expound the issues between Leibniz and Descartes on this topic.

42 In a later defence of 'this method of exclusion' (in reply to Locke's *Examination* of Malebranche's doctrine of seeing all things in God) Leibniz remarked that 'this argument is good if one can completely enumerate the means [of explaining the thing] and exclude all but one'. He agreed with Locke, however, that this preferred hypothesis must explain 'what one would like to understand' and be internally consistent. See Wiener (1951, pp. 497–8). See also Note 27 above.

43 Thus, in *Monadology* §7, he wrote:

There is likewise no way of explaining how a monad can be altered or changed by any other creature, since nothing can be transposed in it, and we cannot conceive in it, *as we can in composite things amongst*

whose parts there may be changes, that any internal motion can be
excited, directed, increased, or diminished from without.
(PPL 643, G vi 607).

44 See, for instance, his *New Essays*, p. 367.
45 See Radner (1985) for a discussion of whether the problem of
interaction was an insuperable one for Descartes.

Text and translation

A student edition should aim to convey Leibniz's thought in clear twentieth-century English that is, as far as possible, intelligible to beginners. For such purposes scholarly considerations are of secondary importance, but it is our belief that, if used with discrimination, scholarship can help achieve this aim.

The manuscript sources for the text of the *Discourse* consist of Leibniz's autograph (Bodemann Theol. III, 1), one complete copy (Bodemann Phil. III, 1 — printed G iv, 327–63) and two partial copies (Bodemann Theol. III, 1). The first copy was checked and revised by Leibniz himself, and nearly every printed edition and translation is based on it. There is something to be said for sticking to the final corrected copy: it can be presumed that this is what most satisfied the author, and philosophers commonly hold that it is the argument that matters, not the historical circumstances. It seems to us, however, that information from the autograph can help us understand Leibniz's position better.

The autograph was first identified and edited around the turn of the century by Henri Lestienne. As usual with Leibniz, it is heavily revised and re-revised — if anything, more so than usual in this case, in view of the importance he attached to it. Lestienne attempted to show, by appropriate typographical conventions every deletion and every addition, so that readers could follow the entire process of drafting from the beginning to the fair copy and revisions of *that*. Some of the resulting variants are no more than incomplete phrases and sentences, and others purely stylistic, or rearrangement of material retained in the final text. But others are more significant. Leibniz can be seen suppressing potentially risky claims and explicit references to other philosophers, enlarging on other matters, changing his examples and qualifying his claims. Some at least of this material seems well suited to helping readers understand Leibniz better and generally making the text clearer.

But how much of this can usefully be offered to English readers is a matter of judgement. A complete rendering of Lestienne's text is out of the question — many of Lestienne's variants are of interest only to scholars, who can in any case consult the original. P. G. Lucas and Leslie Grint, who pursued an ideal of seventeenth-century authenticity we do not share, found evidence of two overall stages of revision for the entire text, and their translation is presented in conformity with this hypothesis. In our judgement, this is excessively conjectural when we do not yet possess a fully critical text of a work that is in any case the product of a few snowbound days in the Harz in early February 1686. We have felt it best to base ourselves on Lestienne's text (supplemented by reference to a microfilm of the autograph) and to make a purely pragmatic selection of those variants that seem useful for elucidating the text, tending on the whole towards generosity rather than to parsimony. We have sought to pick out passages that Leibniz revised heavily; to identify significant suppressions and additions; to help students pick out qualifications that do not affect the structure of the argument; and to help identify the targets of Leibniz's references.

In presenting the rather rich text that results, we have sought to avoid complexity. We have generally, but not invariably, put the first draft in our main text, and identified the later revisions leading to the final version as variants in our apparatus. We hope that this will found easy to follow. Deleted material is shown in square brackets [...], added material between plus signs +...+, and rewritten passages between angle brackets ⟨...⟩, with an explanatory footnote reference. It should be noted, however, that the section summaries (drafted for sending to Arnauld) are all later additions, though not identified as such. In dealing with Leibniz's Biblical quotations, we have been guided by our aim of clear twentieth-century English, and have judged that the New English Bible corresponds to that aim.

R. N. D. M.

Discourse on metaphysics

1. On the divine pefection: God does everything in the most desirable way

The most commonly accepted notion of God we have, and the one most full of meaning, is well enough expressed in these terms: God is an absolutely perfect being. Not enough thought, however, is given to its consequences. If we are to make progress, it is relevant to note that in nature there are several entirely different *perfections, that God possesses them all together, and that each belongs to Him to the highest degree.

We also need to understand what a *perfection is. A sure enough mark of one is that forms or natures not admitting of an ultimate degree are not perfections, as for example the nature of numbers or of shape. For the greatest of all numbers (or rather the number of all numbers), and the greatest of all shapes imply contradictions while omniscience and omnipotence involve no impossibility. Consequently, power and knowledge are perfections, and to the extent that they belong to God, they have no limits.

Hence it follows that since God possesses supreme and infinite wisdom, He acts in the most perfect manner, not only in the metaphysical sense, but also morally speaking. From our point of view we can express ourselves thus: the more we are enlightened and informed about the works of God, the more we shall be disposed to find that they are excellent and satisfactory in every way we could hope.

2. Against those[1] who maintain that there is no goodness in the works of God, or that the rules of goodness and beauty are arbitrary

Thus I am far removed from the opinion of those who maintain that there are no rules of goodness or perfection in the nature of things or in the ideas God has of them, and that the works of God are good only for the formal reason that God made them. For if that were so, +since God knew He was their author,+ He had only to look at them after making them to find them good, in accordance with the testimony of Holy Scripture. But Scripture seems to have made use of this anthropomorphic[2] way of speaking only to make us realise that we recognise the excellence of God's works by considering them by themselves, even when we disregard the purely *extrinsic denomination that refers them to their cause. +This is all the more true in that it is by considering the works that we can discover the Worker, so that the works must carry His marks in themselves.+ I confess that the contrary opinion seems to me extremely dangerous, and very close to the way the ⟨Spinozists⟩[a] think of goodness and harmony.[3] Their opinion is that the beauty of the universe and the goodness we attribute to the works of God are no more than the chimeras of men who conceive God according to their own way of thinking. Also, if we say that things are good by no rule of goodness beyond the will of God alone, we thoughtlessly destroy, I feel, all the love and glory of God. For why praise Him for what He had done if He would be equally praiseworthy for doing the opposite? Where will His justice and His wisdom be, if all that remains of Him is some kind of a despotic power, if His will takes the place of reason, and if, by the very definition of tyranny,[4] what pleases the Almighty is *ipso facto* just? Besides, it seems that every act of willing presupposes some reason for willing, and that reason is naturally prior to will. That is why I still find altogether strange the expression of ⟨Descartes⟩[b] who says that [even] the eternal truths of metaphysics and geometry[, and consequently also the rules of goodness, justice and perfection] are no more than the effects of God's will.[5] It seems to me, rather, that they are no more than the consequences of His understanding, which certainly does not depend on His will, any more His essence does.

a. later changed to 'the latest *innovators'.

b. later changed to 'certain other philosophers'.

3.   Against those who think God could have done better

Neither can I approve the opinion of some ⟨scholastics⟩[a] who maintain boldly that what God has done is not absolutely perfect, and that He could have done much better. For it seems to me that the consequences of this opinion are altogether contrary to the glory of God. 'Just as the lesser evil contains a proportion of good, so the lesser good contains a proportion of evil.'[6] To act with less perfection than one could have done is to act imperfectly. To show that an architect could have done better is to find fault with his work. It also runs counter to the assurance of the goodness of God's works in Holy Scripture. For, since perfections decrease to infinity, however God did his work, it would always [be] good in comparison with the less perfect, if that were enough. But a thing is not very praiseworthy if it is only so in that way. I also think that a very large number of passages favouring my opinion could be found in the divine Scriptures and the holy Fathers, with scarcely any favouring that of those ⟨new scholastics⟩[b] + − a view unknown, in my opinion, to the whole of antiquity. It is based on our insufficient knowledge of the general harmony of the universe and of the hidden reasons for God's conduct which lead us to the rash judgement that many things could have been done better+. Besides, these moderns insist on some subtleties that are not very sound, for they imagine that nothing is so perfect but that there is something that is more perfect, which is a mistake. [There is an infinity of regular figures, but one is the most perfect, namely the circle. If a triangle had to be made and there was no further specification of the kind of triangle, God would assuredly make an equilateral triangle because, absolutely speaking, that is the most perfect.]

They also think that in this way they are providing for the liberty of God, as if it were not the highest liberty to act in accordance with sovereign reason. For, apart from its apparent impossibility, the belief that God acts in some matter without any reason for His act of will is hardly consistent with His glory. Suppose, for example, that God chooses between A and B, and that He takes A without any reason for preferring it to B; I say that that action of God would at the least not be praiseworthy. For every praise must be based on some reason and here *ex hypothesi* there is none. On the contrary, I hold that God does nothing for which He does not merit being glorified.

a.   later changed to 'moderns'.

b.   later changed to 'moderns'.

4. **Loving God demands complete satisfaction with and acquiescence in what He does, but we do not, on that account, have to be *quietists**

The general recognition of this great truth – that God always acts in the most perfect and desirable manner possible – is to my mind the basis of the love we owe to God concerning all things. For he who loves seeks his satisfaction in the happiness or perfection of the loved one and his actions. 'True friendship is to want the same and to reject the same'.[7] And I think that it is difficult to love God well when not disposed to will what He wills, if changing that were in our power. Indeed those who are not satisfied with what He does seem to me like discontented subjects +[of a king or of a republic]+ whose intentions are little different from those of rebels.

Hence, in accordance with these principles, I hold that to act in conformity with the love of God it is not enough to be patient under duress. We must be truly satisfied with all that happens to us in consequence of His will. I mean this acquiescence to apply to the past. As far as the future is concerned, we must not be *quietists nor wait ridiculously with arms folded for what God will do, in accordance with the sophism the Ancients called λόγον 'άεγον +lazy reason+. On the contrary, we must act in accordance with the presumptive will of God, as far as we can judge it, trying with all our ability to contribute to the general good, especially to the adornment and perfection of what concerns us or is near us, or, so to speak, within our range. For when the outcome shows that God may perhaps not want our good will to have its effect for the present, it does not follow that He does not want us to do what we have done. On the contrary, since He is the best of all masters, He never asks for more than the right intentions, and it is for Him to know the hour and the place for bringing good plans to fruition.

5. **What are the rules of perfection of God's conduct; and that the simplicity of means is balanced by the richness of effects**

Hence it is enough to have this confidence in God, that He does everything for the best and that nothing can harm those who love him. But to know in detail the reasons that could have moved Him to choose this *order of the universe, to allow sins, or to dispense

His saving grace in a particular way, is beyond the power of a finite mind, particularly of a finite mind that has not yet attained enjoyment of the sight of God.

Nevertheless, some general remarks can be made on the conduct of Providence in the government of things. Thus it can be said that [whatever encloses more reality in less volume is more perfect], that he who acts perfectly is like an excellent geometer who knows how to find the best constructions for a problem; +like a good architect who arranges his site and the funds intended for the building in the most advantageous manner, so as to leave nothing that jars or lacks the beauty of which it is capable; like a good householder who uses his property so that nothing is left uncultivated or barren;+ like a skilled engineer who achieves his result by the least complicated way that could be chosen; like an experienced author who includes as much reality as he is able in the least space. Now the most *perfect of all beings, occupying the least volume, in other words, those which hinder the least, are minds, and their perfections are the virtues. That is why we must not doubt that the happiness of minds is the principal objective of God and that He pursues it as much as the general harmony allows. More will be said of this presently.

+As for the simplicity of God's ways, that applies properly in respect of means whereas the variety, richness or abundance applies to aims or effects. The one has to be in balance with the other, like the expenses of a building with the size and beauty expected of it. It is true that nothing costs God anything, much less than it costs a philosopher to make hypotheses for the construction of his imaginary world, since God has only to make decrees to bring a real world to birth; but in relation to wisdom, in so far as they are mutually independent, decrees or hypotheses take the place of expenditure, for reason demands that we avoid a multiplicity of hypotheses or principles; in almost the same way the simplest *system is always preferred in astronomy.+

6. God does nothing out of order and it is not even possible to imagine events that are not regular

The decisions or actions of God are commonly divided into ordinary and extraordinary. But it is well to bear in mind that God does nothing out of order. So, whatever passes for extraordinary is only so in relation to some particular order established among creatures. For, in relation to the universal order, everything conforms to it. So true is this, that not only does nothing happen in the world that is absolutely irregular, but such a thing cannot even be imagined. Suppose, for example, that someone puts a number of points on paper completely at random like those who practise the ridiculous art of geomancy[8], then I say that it is possible to find a geometric line whose notion is constant and uniform according to some rule, so that this line passes through all these points and does so in the same order as they were made by the hand.

And if someone were to draw in one movement a line that was sometimes straight, sometimes circular, and sometimes of some other kind, it is possible to find a notion, a rule, or an equation common to all the points in that line and in virtue of which these same changes had to occur. +For example there is no face whose contour is not part of a geometric line and cannot be drawn all in one movement by some rule-governed motion.+ But when a rule is very complicated, what conforms to it is taken to be irregular.

Thus it can be said that however God might have created the world, it would always have been regular and within some general order. But God chose that world that is the most perfect, i.e. the one that is simultaneously the simplest in hypotheses and richest in phenomena, just as a geometric line might be if its construction was easy but its properties most admirable and extensive. +I make use of these comparisons to sketch some kind of imperfect resemblance to the divine wisdom and to say something that could at least raise our minds to conceive in some way what cannot be adequately expressed. But by this I do not claim to explain the great mystery on which the whole universe depends.+

7. **Miracles conform to the general order although they are contrary to *subaltern norms. What God wishes or permits by a general or particular will**

Now, since nothing can take place that is not within the *order, it can be said that miracles are just as much within the order as natural operations, are so called because they conform to certain *subaltern norms we call the nature of things. For it can be said that this 'nature' is no more than a custom of God from which He can exempt Himself in virtue of a stronger reason than the one that moved Him to make use of these norms.

As for the general and particular wills,[9] depending on how we take the matter, it can be said that God does everything in accordance with His +most+ general will, the one in conformity with the most perfect order He chose. But it can also be said that He has particular wills, which are exceptions to the subaltern norms mentioned above; for the most general of the laws of God, by means of which He regulates the whole universe, are without exception.

+It can also be said that God wills everything that is an object of His particular will. But as for the objects of His general will, such as the actions of other creatures, particularly of those that are rational, and with which {i.e. the *actions*} God wishes to concur, we must draw a distinction: if the action is good in itself, it can be said that God wills it and sometimes commands it, even when it does not happen; but if it is evil in itself, and only becomes good by accident, it has to be said that God permits it and not that He wills it, though He *concurs in it through the laws of nature established by Him, and because he is able to draw from it greater good. This comes about because the *sequence of things, particularly punishment and recompense, corrects its evil nature, and compensates for the evil with interest, so that in the end there is more perfection in all that follows than if none of the evil had happened.+

8. In order to distinguish the actions of God from those of creatures, an explanation is given of the notion of an individual substance

It is rather difficult to distinguish the actions of God from those of creatures [as well as the actions and passions of these same creatures]. For there are those who think that God does everything,[10] while others imagine that He does no more than conserve the force He has given to creatures.[11] +What follows will show how far either of these can be said.+ Now since, properly speaking, actions belong to individual substances ('actions belong to *supposita*'[12]), it will be necessary to explain just what such a substance is.

⟨It seems to me⟩[a] that when several predications are attributed to the same subject and this subject is not attributed to any other, this subject is called an individual substance. But that is not enough and such an explanation is merely *nominal, so we need to consider what it is to be truly attributed to a particular subject.

Now it is acknowledged that all true predication has some basis in the nature of things, and when a proposition is not an identity, that is, when the predicate is not expressly included in the subject, it must be so included virtually. That is what the Philosophers call *inesse+, when they say that the predicate is in the subject+. Thus the subject term must always include that of the predicate, so that whoever understood the notion of the subject perfectly would also judge that the predicate belongs to it.

That being so, we can say that the nature of an individual substance or *complete being is to have such a *complete notion as to include and entail all the predicates of the subject that notion is attributed to. In contrast, an accident is a being whose notion does not include all that can be attributed to the subject it is attributed to. Thus the circular figure of the ring of Gyges^b, does not contain everything that makes up the individual notion of this ring. Whereas God sees in it at the same time the foundation and cause for all the predicates that can truly be applied to it, such as that it would be swallowed by a fish and nevertheless returned to its master. I speak here as if this ring were a substance.

a.   Revised in MS to begin 'It is indeed true'.

b.   Text as for first draft. The example was later changed to Alexander the Great, and after much amendment the text finally read: 'Thus the quality of being king that belongs to Alexander the Great, taken in abstraction from the subject, is not sufficiently determinate for one individual, and does not include the other qualities of the same subject, nor everything that the notion of this prince includes, whereas God who sees the individual notion or haecceity^13 of Alexander sees in it at the same time the foundation and reason for all the predicates that can truly be ascribed to him, such as that he would defeat Darius and Porus even to the point of knowing *a priori (and not by experience) whether he died naturally or by poison, something we can only know historically. Also, when we consider well the *connection of things, we can say that there is in the soul of Alexander for all time traces of everything that happened to him, and marks of everything that will happen to him, and even traces of everything happening in the universe, though to recognise them all belongs to God alone.'

9. **Each unique substance expresses the whole universe in its own way, and included in its notion are all the events that happen to it with all their circumstances, and the whole sequence of external things**

Among several *paradoxical conclusions following from this, is that it is not true that two substances are completely alike, differing only numerically+, and what St Thomas has to say on this point about angels and intelligences ('in these cases every individual is a *lowest species'¹⁴) is true of all substances provided that the specific *difference is taken in the way geometers take it in relation to their figures+. [Likewise, if bodies are substances,¹⁵ their natures cannot possibly consist solely in size, figure and motion: something else is needed.] Likewise, a substance can begin only by creation and perish only by annihilation; a substance cannot be divided into two, nor can two substances become one, and so the number of substances does not naturally increase or diminish, though they are frequently transformed.

Moreover every substance +is as it were an entire world and a *mirror of God, or rather of the whole universe, *expressing it in its own way, somewhat as the same town is variously represented according to the different positions of an observer. It can even be said that every substance+ bears in some way the mark of the infinite wisdom and omnipotence of God, imitating Him as far as it is capable. For it expresses, if only confusedly, all that happens in the universe, past, present and future, and this has some resemblance to an infinite perception or knowledge. And since all other substances in turn express it +and are accommodated to it+, it can be said to extend its power over all the others in imitation of the omnipotence of the Creator.

10. **There is some soundness to the belief in *substantial forms, but these make no difference to the phenomena, and should not be used to explain particular effects**

It seems that the ancients [in distinguishing an *ens per se* from an *ens per accidens* and in introducing *substantial forms], as well as the many able people who were accustomed to profound meditations and who taught theology and philosophy centuries ago, many of them praiseworthy for their sanctity, had some knowledge of what we have just said. This is what led them to introduce and uphold the substantial forms so much in disfavour today. But they are neither so far from the truth nor as ridiculous as the common run of our *modern philosophers imagine.

I agree that the knowledge of forms is of no use in the details of physics and should not be used for explaining the particulars of phenomena. That is where our *scholastics went wrong, and with them the physicians of the past who followed their example, in thinking to account for the properties of bodies by mentioning forms and qualities without taking the trouble to examine their manner of operation. It is as if we were to content ourselves with saying that a clock has the horodictic quality deriving from its form without considering what that consists in. +That indeed might be enough for whoever buys the clock, provided he left its maintenance to someone else+.

But this shortcoming and misuse of forms should not make us reject something whose knowledge is so necessary in metaphysics that without it, I hold, the first principles cannot be well understood, nor the mind sufficiently raised to the knowledge of incorporeal natures and the wonders of God.

Nevertheless, a geometer has no need to trouble his mind with the famous labyrinth of the composition of the *continuum+, and neither has any moral philosopher, and still less any legal expert or politician, any need to trouble himself with the great difficulties involved in reconciling the freedom of the will with the providence of God+. For the geometer can complete all his demonstrations +and the politician conclude all his deliberations+ without entering into these discussions, importance as they are in philosophy +and theology+. In the same way, a physicist can account for experiments, sometimes by means of simpler experiments carried out before, and sometimes by means of geometrical and *mechanical demonstrations, without the need of forms and other general considerations belonging to another sphere. If he employs the [extraordinary] *concurrence of God, or some soul, *arché or other thing of that nature, he is wandering as far off course[16] as he who tries to introduce the nature of destiny and our liberty into a deliberation about an important practical matter.

Men often make this mistake without thinking when they trouble their minds by considering fate, and sometimes they are even diverted from some good resolution or necessary care as a result.

11. The meditations of the theologians and philosophers called '*scholastics' are not to be despised entirely

I know that in claiming in some way to rehabilitate the old philosophy and restore the all but banished *substantial forms [to which not enough justice has been done] to life, I am proposing a big *paradox. [But I only do this on the supposition that it is possible to speak of bodies as substances.] But perhaps I shall not be lightly condemned if it is known that I have long meditated on modern philosophy, and spent much time on physical experiments and geometrical demonstrations, and that I was long persuaded of the vanity of such beings. But I was eventually obliged to take them up again against my will and as if by force. It was as a result of carrying out my own researches that I was made to recognise that our moderns do not do full justice to St Thomas and other great men of those times, and that the opinions of scholastic philosophers and theologians are much more sound than is imagined, as long as they are used appropriately and in their place. I am even convinced that if some exact and reflecting mind took the trouble to clarify and digest their thoughts in the manner of *analytical geometry, he would find a treasure store of very important truths which could be demonstrated completely.

12. Notions defined by extension involve something imaginary and cannot constitute the essence of bodies

But, to take up again the thread of our considerations, I believe that any one who meditates on the nature of substance as I have explained it above will find that either bodies are not substances in strict metaphysical rigour (the view indeed of the *Platonists), or that the whole nature of body does not consist solely in extension, i.e. in size, shape and motion. On the contrary, something related to souls which is commonly called a '*substantial form' has necessarily to be recognised in them, though that makes no more difference to the phenomena than the souls of animals, if they have any[17]. It can even be demonstrated that the notions of size, shape and motion are not so distinct as is imagined and that they involve something imaginary and relative to our perceptions, just as colour, heat and other similar qualities also do, +(to an even greater extent)+ — we may doubt that these are truly in the nature of external things. That is why qualities of these kinds could not constitute any substance. And if there were no other principle of identity in body that the one just considered, no body would ever last more than a moment.[18]

+Nevertheless, souls and substantial forms of other bodies are very different from intelligent souls, who alone know what they do, and which not only do not naturally perish but even for ever retain the basis of the knowledge of what they are. This makes them liable to punishment and reward, and makes them citizens of the republic of the universe whose monarch is God. It also follows that all other creatures ought to serve them, something we shall discuss more fully presently.+[19]

13. **Since the individual notion of every person includes once for all everything that will ever happen to him, in it are to be seen the *a priori proofs of each event, or rather why one happened rather than the other. But although these truths are assured, they do not cease to be contingent, since they are based on the free will of God or of creatures. There are always reasons for their choices but these incline without necessitating**

But a great difficulty can arise from the foundations laid above, and before proceeding further, we must try to deal with it. We said that the notion of an individual substance includes once for all everything that can ever happen to it, and that by considering this notion, we can see in it everything that can truly be stated about it, just as we can see in the nature of the circle all the properties that can be derived from it. But from that it seems [that all events will become fatally necessary] that the difference between necessary and contingent truths will be destroyed, [that all the fate of the *Stoics will take the place of liberty,] there will no longer be any room for human liberty, and absolute fate will reign over all our actions as well as over all other events in the world. My reply is: we must distinguish between what is certain and what is necessary.

Everyone agrees that future contingents are assured since God foresees them, but it is not for all that admitted that they are necessary. But (it will be said) if some conclusion can be infallibly deduced from a definition or notion will be necessary. Now in fact we do maintain that everything that is to happen to a person is already included virtually in his nature or notion, just as the properties of a circle are included in its definition. +So the difficulty remains.+ In order to give a sound answer, I claim that connection or derivation is of two kinds: one is absolutely necessary (its contrary implies a contradiction) and occurs with eternal truths like those of geometry; the other is necessary only *ex hypothesi*, by accident, so to speak, but in itself it is contingent, since its contrary does not imply a contradiction. This connection is based, not on the absolutely pure ideas and God's bare understanding alone, but also on His free decrees +and the *connection of the universe+.

Let us take an example. Since Peter[a] will deny our Lord, that action is included in his notion, for we are supposing it to be in the nature of such a perfect notion to include everything, so that the predicate should be included in it, *ut possit *inesse subjecto.*[20] We could say that it is not in virtue of this notion or idea or nature that he must sin, since that only applies to him because God knows everything. But, it will be insisted, his nature or form corresponds to his notion. I reply that it is indeed true and since God imposed this personality on him he must henceforth conform to it. +I could reply with the objection of future contingents, for these have as yet no reality outside the understanding and the will, and since God gave them this form in advance, they will have to conform to it all the same.+

+But I prefer to deal with difficulties than make excuses for them with examples of some other similar difficulties, and what I am going to say will help clarify both.+ Thus it is here that we must apply the distinction between the kinds of connection. I say that +what happens+ in accordance with these prior conditions is assured, but that it is not necessary; and if he did the opposite, he would be doing nothing impossible +in itself though it would be *ex hypothesi* impossible that this should happen+. For if someone were capable of completing the whole of the demonstration by virtue of which he proved the connection between the subject Peter and the predicate (namely, his denial), he would show that this fact had its basis in his notion or nature, and that it was reasonable and consequently assured that it should come about; but he would not show that it was necessary in itself, nor that its contrary implied a contradiction. In almost the same way, it is reasonable and assured that God will always do the best, although what is less perfect involves no contradiction [in itself].

For it would be found that this demonstration of this predicate of Peter is not as absolute as those of numbers and geometry, but that it supposes the *sequence of things freely chosen by God and founded on the first free decree of God, which always leads him to do what is most perfect, as well as on the decree God made (in consequence of the first) concerning human nature, which is that man will always (although freely) do what seems best. Now every truth founded on decrees of this kind is contingent, although certain, since those decrees make no difference to the possibility of things and, as I have already said, although God assuredly always chooses the best, that does not prevent what is less perfect remaining possible in itself, though it does not happen. It is not its impossibility but its imperfection that causes it to be rejected. Nothing is necessary if its contrary is possible.

+Hence, we are in a position to meet such difficulties, great as they may appear to be (and indeed they are no less pressing for all others who have ever dealt with this matter,)+ provided it is fully realised that contingent propositions have reasons for being that way rather than otherwise, or (what comes to the same thing) that there are *a priori* proofs of their truth which make them certain and show that the subject-predicate connection in these propositions has its basis in the nature of each. But these are not necessary demonstrations, since these reasons are only based +on the principle of the contingency or of the existence of things, i.e. +on what is or seems to be the best of several equally possible things; whereas necessary truths are founded on the principle of contradiction and on the possibility or impossibility of the essences themselves, without regard to the free will of God or of creatures.

a. Example later expanded and changed to Julius Caesar's becoming perpetual dictator and master of the republic and taking away the liberty of the Romans.

14. God produces different substances according to the different views he has of the universe. The distinctive nature of each substance ensures, by the ⟨mediation⟩ᵃ of God, that what happens to each corresponds to what happens to all the others, without them acting directly on each other.

Having after a fashion come to know what the nature of [created] substances consists in, we must try to explain their mutual dependence and their actions and *passions. Now, in the first place, it is altogether obvious that created substances depend on God who conserves them — and even continually produces them by a kind of *emanation, as we do our thoughts. For as God, so to speak, turns on all its sides and in all ways the general *system of phenomena which He finds it good to produce to manifest His glory, and as He looks at all the faces of the world in all possible ways – because there is no relation that escapes His omniscience – the result of each view of the universe as if seen from a particular place is a substance expressing the universe in conformity with that view, if God finds it good to make His thought effective and produce this substance. And since the view of God is always true, our perceptions are so too; it is those of our judgements that derive from us that deceive us.

+Now we have said above, and it follows from what we have just said, that+ each substance is like a world on its own, independent of everything else apart from God. Hence all our *phenomena, that is, all that can ever happen to us, are consequences of our natures [and, since we are free substances, of our wills]. Since these phenomena preserve a particular order +conforming to our nature or, so to speak, the world within us,+ so that we are able +(to make observations useful for regulating our conduct which are justified by the favourable outcome of future phenomena)+ and to judge the future by the past without error, this enables us to say that these *phenomena are true, without worrying +whether they are outside us or+ whether others perceive them as well. Nevertheless, it is very true that the perceptions or ⟨qualities⟩ᵇ of all substances correspond with each other, so that each, carefully following the particular reasons or laws it has observed, fits in with the other +in doing the same, just as when several people agree with each other to be at a particular

place at a prearranged day, they can in fact do so if they wish+.
+Now although all express the same phenomena, +it does not
follow from this that their *expressions should be perfectly
similar: it is enough that they are proportionate to each other. In
the same way several spectators think they have seen the same thing
+and indeed agree with each other+, although each sees and
speaks according to his point of view.

Now it is God from whom all ⟨substances⟩ᶜ *emanate continually +and He sees the universe, not only as they see it, but quite
differently from them all as well+. He is the only cause of this
correspondence between their *phenomena, and He alone makes
what is peculiar to one public to all+, otherwise there would be no
connection between them+. Hence it can be said +in a manner
of speaking and in a sense that is good, though remote from
ordinary usage+ that a particular substance never acts on another
particular substance and is not acted upon by another either. This
follows if we remember that what happens to each is only a
consequence of its idea or ⟨*complete notion⟩ᵈ alone, since that
idea+ already includes all the predicates or events, and+ expresses
the whole universe. Indeed, nothing can happen to us but thoughts
and perceptions, and +all our thoughts+ and our future
perceptions are no more than consequences, albeit contingent, +of
our previous thoughts and perceptions. Hence, if I were capable of
considering distinctly everything happening or appearing to me at
the present time, I would be able to see therein everything that
would ever happen or appear to me. +This would not fail, but
would happen in any case, if everything outside me were
destroyed and only God and myself remained.+ But as we
attribute to other things+, as if to causes acting on us, +what we
perceive in some way in other things, we have to consider the basis
of this judgement, and what truth there is in it.

[It is above all agreed that if we desire some phenomenon to
happen at a certain time and it occurs in the ordinary course of
things, we say that we acted and that we were the cause of it, as
when I want to, as we say, 'move my hand'. Also, when it seems
to me that by my will something happens to what I call another
substance (and that this is the way it would happen as I judge from
frequent observation) although it was not willed by it, I judge
that this substance is acted upon. I admit this of myself when
something happens to me in accordance with the will of another

substance. Also, when we will something to happen, and something else follows from it that we did not want, we still say that we did it, provided that we understood how it followed. There are also some phenomena of extension that we attribute to ourselves more particularly and which have their basis *a parte rei* in what is called our body. As everything of importance happening to it (i.e. all the notable changes appearing to us in it) make themselves strongly felt in it, ordinarily at least, we attribute all the *passions to this body to ourselves. We do so with very good reason, for even if we did not perceive them at the time, we do not fail to become well aware of the consequences, just as if we had been transported from one place to another while asleep. We also attribute to ourselves the actions of this body, as when we run, hit or fall, and when our body, continuing the motion once begun, has some effect. But I do not attribute to myself what happens to other bodies, because I realise that great changes can happen that I cannot perceive, unless my body is exposed to them in a way I conceive appropriate to that assumption.

So it is quite clear that although all the bodies of the universe belong to us in some way and harmonise with ours, we do not attribute to ourselves what happens to them. For when my body is pushed, I say that I myself have been pushed, but if someone else is pushed, I do not say that I have been pushed, even though I may perceive it and some *passion in me may arise from it, since I measure where I am by the place my body is in. And this language is highly reasonable because it is appropriate for clear expression in everyday practice. As for the mind, it can be said briefly that our acts of will and judgements or reasonings are actions while our perceptions or sensations are *passions. As for the body, we say that a change that happens to it is an action when it follows from a previous change, but otherwise it is a passion.

In general, to give our terms a meaning that reconciles metaphysics with practice, it can be said that when several powers are affected by the same change the one that passes to a higher degree of perfection or continues in the same acts, while the one that immediately becomes more limited thereby, so that its expressions become more confused, is acted upon.]ᵉ

a. Revised in MS to read 'intervention'.

b. Revised in MS to read '*expressions'.

c. Revised in MS to read 'individuals'.

d. At various stages Leibniz tried 'nature' and '*essence'.

e. Entire three paragraphs removed before copying.

15. The action of one finite substance on another consists solely in the increase in the degree of its *expression together with the diminution of that of the other, in so far as God has made them conform to each other.

But without getting involved in a long discussion, it is enough for the present to reconcile the language of metaphysics with that of practice by noting that we attribute to ourselves [our more clear and distinct perceptions and that we can in general attribute to a substance its more clear and distinct expression] +and, with reason, the *phenomena we express more perfectly, while we attribute to other substances what each best expresses. Thus a substance of infinite extension, in so far as it expresses everything, becomes limited by its more or less perfect manner of *expression. Thus in this way it is possible to conceive that substances mutually hinder or limit each other and, consequently, in this sense, to say that they act on each other and, so to speak, are obliged to conform to each other. For it can happen that a change which increases the *expression of the one diminishes that of the other. Now, the virtue of a particular substance is to express well the glory of God, and it is there that it is least limited, and everything that exerts its virtue or power, that is when it acts, changes for the better and is *extended in so far as it acts.+ Thus when a change affects several substances (since indeed every change touches all of them), I think that it can be said that the one that thereby passes to a higher degree of perfection +or to a more perfect expression exerts its power and+ acts, while the other one that passes to a lesser degree +shows its weakness and+ is acted upon. So I hold that every action +of a substance possessing perception+ implies some pleasure and every passion some pain, and *vice versa*. This notwithstanding that it can easily happen that a present advantage is destroyed in what follows. +Hence it follows that it is possible to sin by acting or exerting one's power and finding pleasure therein.+

16. The extraordinary *concurrence of God is included in the *expression of our *essence because it applies to everything, but it transcends the powers of our nature of distinct expression (which is finite and follows particular subaltern norms)

All that remains for the present is to explain how it is sometimes possible for God to have influence on men +or other substances+ through an extraordinary or miraculous *concurrence, since it seems that ⟨everything that has to happen to them is natural in so far as it is a consequence of their substance.⟩ᵃ But what we said above about miracles in the universe must be remembered:²¹ they always conform to the universal laws of the general order, even though these transcend the subordinate norms. And, to the extent that every person +or substance+ is like a little world expressing the great one, it can even be said that ⟨this extraordinary concurrence of God is included in the general order of the universe in so far as that is expressed by the nature of this person, but it does not cease to be miraculous and to be beyond the norms⟩.ᵇ +That is why, if everything it expresses is included in our nature, nothing is supernatural with respect to it, for it *extends to everything, since an effect always expresses its cause and God is the true cause of substances. But since what our nature expresses more perfectly particularly belongs to it, that is what its power consists in — and since, as I have just explained, it is limited, there are many things that surpass the powers of our natures, and even those of every limited nature. Consequently, to speak more clearly,+ I say that miracles and the extraordinary acts of God's concurrence have the particular character that they could not be foreseen by the reasoning of any created mind, however enlightened it might be, since the comprehension of the general order surpasses them all, while everything called natural depends on the less general norms creatures can understand. Hence, in order ⟨to say nothing of these norms or laws of nature that might cause offence⟩,ᶜ it would be good to link particular ways of speaking with particular thoughts: whatever includes everything we express could then be called our essence +or idea+, and since it expresses our union with God, it has no limits and nothing exceeds it. But what is limited in us could be called our nature or power, and in this respect what exceeds the natures of all created substances is supernatural.

a.   Revised in MS to read: 'nothing extraordinary or supernatural could happen to them, since all their events are only consequences of their natures'.

b.   Revised in MS to read: 'this extraordinary action of God on this substance does not cease to be miraculous although it is included in the general *order of the universe to the extent that it is expressed by the *essence or individual notion of this substance.'

c.   Revised in MS to read: 'that the words should be as unobjectionable as their sense'.

17.   Example of a *subaltern norm or law of nature; in which it is shown that God always preserves the same force, but not the same quantity of motion ... against the Cartesians and some others

I have often mentioned *subaltern maxims or laws of nature already, and it would be good to give an example. Our new philosophers commonly make use of that famous rule [advanced by Descartes] that God always preserves the same quantity of motion in the world. It ⟨seems⟩ᵃ highly plausible indeed, and in the past I held it to be indubitable. But I have since come to recognise wherein lay its error. It is that Descartes and many other able mathematicians thought that the quantity of motion (i.e. the speed times the size of the mobile) ⟨was the same thing as the force, or at least expressed it perfectly⟩ᵇ, +or geometrically speaking, that the forces are in compound proportion of the speeds and the bodies+. Now it is ⟨obvious⟩ᶜ indeed that the same force should always be preserved in the universe. So, when we attend to the phenomena with care, we see clearly that mechanical perpetual motion does not occur, because then the force of a machine+, which is continually being slightly diminished by friction, and must consequently soon cease,+ would be replaced and so would increase of itself without any new impulsion from outside. We also note that the force of a body is diminished solely to the extent that it gives some of it to +neighbouring +bodies +or to its own parts in so far as these have independent motions+.

Thus they thought that what can be said of force could also be said of quantity of motion. But, to show the difference, I suppose that a body falling from a particular height acquires the force needed to climb up again, if its direction of travel should take it that way+, unless there are hindrances+. For example, a pendulum would rise right back again to the height it had fallen from if the resistance of the air and other small obstacles did not somehow diminish the force acquired.

I suppose also that as much force is needed to raise a body A of one pound a height CD of four fathoms as to raise a body B of four pounds a height EF of one fathom. [See page 84.] All this is accepted by our new philosophers.

Hence, it is manifest that body (A), after falling from the height CD has acquired as much force precisely as body (B) after falling from the height EF. +For when body (B) has arrived at F and has the force to climb back to E (by the first supposition), it has in consequence the force to carry a body of four pounds, that is its own body, to the height EF of one fathom, and similarly, when body (A) has reached D and has the force to climb back to C, it has the force to carry a body of one pound, that is its own body, to the height CD of four fathoms. Hence (by the second supposition), the forces of the two bodies are equal.+

Now let us see whether the quantity of motion is also the same in both cases: but it is here that there will be surprise at finding a very great difference. For it has been demonstrated by Galileo that the speed acquired in the fall CD is twice that acquired in the fall EF, though the height is quadruple. If then, we multiply the body (A), in the proportion 1, by the speed, in the proportion 2, the product +or quantity of motion+ will be as 2, and if on the other hand, we multiply the body (B), which is as 4, by its speed, which is as 1, then the product or quantity of motion will be as 4. Hence the quantity of motion of body (A) at point D is half the quantity of motion of body (B) at point F, though their forces are equal +. Hence there is a great difference between the quantity of motion and the force+, as was to be proved.

+From this it is seen that the force must be measured by the quantity of the effect it can produce, e.g. by the height to which a heavy body of a particular size and kind can be raised, something very different from the speed that can be given it, and that to give it twice the speed more than twice the force is needed.+

Nothing is simpler than this proof. Descartes only fell into error here because he trusted too much in his thoughts before they had matured enough [with a confidence based on the happy success of some of his thoughts and on his experience of the penetration of his mind, which rendered him rather too rash in the end]. But I am astonished that his followers have not recognised this error since, and I fear that little by little they begin to imitate the *Peripatetics they so make fun of, and that like them they grow accustomed to consulting the books of their master rather than reason and nature.

a.   Amended in MS to read 'is'.

b.   Amended in MS to read 'was completely adequate to the motive force'.

c.   Amended in MS to read 'reasonable'.

18.   **Importance of the distinction between force and quantity of motion *inter alia* in deciding that we must have recourse to metaphysical considerations distinct from extension to explain the ⟨nature⟩ᵃ of bodies.**

This consideration of the distinction of force from quantity of motion is important enough, not only in +physics and mechanics+ in the discovery of the true laws of nature and rules of motions+, and even in the correction of several practical errors that have slipped into the writings of some able mathematicians,+ but also in metaphysics, in the better understanding of the principles [of things]. For motion+, if its precise formal content only — i.e. change of place — is considered,+ is not a completely real thing, and when several bodies mutually exchange their places, it is impossible to determine from these changes alone which of them ought to have motion or rest attributed to it+, as I could show geometrically if I wanted to dwell on this point now+.

But the force or direct cause of these changes is something more real, and there is ⟨some⟩ᵇ basis for attributing it to one body rather than to another, and it is only thereby that we can know which one the motion is best attributed to. Now, this force is something different from size and motion, and it can be concluded from this that what is conceived in bodies does not consist solely in extension and its modifications, contrary to the conviction of our moderns. Hence, too, we are obliged to re-establish some of the beings or forms banished by them. And although all the particular phenomena of [corporeal] nature can be explained mathematically or mechanically by those who understand them, it nevertheless appears more and more that the general principles of corporeal mechanical nature itself are metaphysical rather than geometrical, belonging to forms or indivisible natures functioning as causes of the ⟨matter or extension⟩ᶜ rather than to corporeal or extended mass — a reflection capable of reconciling +the *mechanical philosophy of the moderns with the circumspection of+ some intelligent well-intentioned people who fear quite reasonably that we are moving too far from immaterial beings to the disadvantage of piety.

a. Amended in MS to 'phenomena'.

b. Amended in MS to 'a sufficient'.

c. Amended in MS to 'phenomena'.

19. Usefulness of final causes in physics

As I do not like to judge ⟨people's intentions, or only do so favourably if I can⟩,ᵃ I am not accusing our new philosophers [of impiety] when they claim to banish final causes in physics. Nevertheless I am obliged to admit that [I do not recognise their usual intelligence and prudence therein and that] +the consequences of this opinion seem dangerous to me, particularly when it is connected with that refuted by me at the beginning of this discourse, which seems to lead to their removal altogether, as if God never had any aim, whether good or active, or as if the good were not the object of His will ... +For my part, I hold on the contrary that it is just there that we have to seek the principle of all existences and [even] of the laws of nature, since God always intends what is best and most perfect.

I am happy to admit that we are liable to error when we want to determine the aims and counsels of God, but that is only when we try to restrict them to a particular plan, in the belief that He has only one single thing in view, whereas in fact He considers everything at once. +Thus, when we think that God made the world for us alone, we are greatly mistaken, although it is true that

He made it in its totality for us and that there is nothing in the world that does not affect us and does not also conform to His concerns for us, in accordance with the above principles.+ Thus, when we see some good effect or perfection happening or resulting from the works of God, we can certainly say that God intended it, for He +does nothing by chance and+ unlike us does not sometimes fail to do well. That is why, far from being in an error here, +akin to that of the overly political who attribute excessive refinement to the designs of princes, or to that of commentators who search for too much erudition in their authors, we cannot attribute too many reflections to this infinite Wisdom, and+ there is no matter in which there is less danger of error as long as we only affirm and avoid negative propositions here that limit the plans of God.

Everyone who sees the admirable structure of animals is led to recognise the wisdom of the Author of things, and I advise those with any feeling of piety+ or even of true Philosophy+ to avoid the expression of some would-be tough minds who say that we see because we +happen to+ have eyes, without noting that the eyes were made to see. If we are seriously involved in these opinions that assign everything to the necessity of matter or to a particular chance (although both must seem ridiculous to those who understand what we have explained above), ⟨we will inevitably fail to⟩[b] recognise an intelligent Author of nature. ⟨For it is ridiculous to introduce a Sovereign Intelligence as the Ordainer of things and not use His wisdom to account for phenomena.⟩[c] As if, in accounting for the conquest of a great prince in capturing an important position, a historian tried to say that it was because the particles of the gunpowder liberated by lighting the fuse escaped at a speed +capable of pushing a hard heavy body against the walls of the position+, while the branches of the particles+ composing the copper of the cannon+ were sufficiently intertwined not to be separated by this speed, instead of showing how the foresight of the victor caused him to choose the appropriate time and means, and how his power overcame all the obstacles.

a.   Amended in MS to 'judge people in a hostile way'.

b.   Amended in MS to 'it will be difficult to'.

c.   Amended in MS to 'For the effect must answer to its cause and is even best known through the knowledge of its cause, and it is unreasonable after introducing a Sovereign Intelligence ordering things, to go on, instead of then making use of His wisdom, to use the properties of matter alone in explaining the phenomena.'

20.   Remarkable passage of Socrates in Plato against +excessively materialistic philosophers+

This point reminds me of a fine passage of Socrates in Plato's *Phaedo*. In marvellous agreement with my thoughts on this point, it seems to be written expressly against our excessively materialistic philosophers. So this account made me want to translate it, and though it is rather long, perhaps this sample will give one of us the occasion to share many other fine sound thoughts from the writings of the great man.[22]

'One day', he said, 'I heard someone read a book of Anaxagoras, where there were these words "that an Intelligent Being was the cause of all things, and that He arranged and adorned them". I was extremely pleased with that, for I thought that if the world was the result of an Intelligence, everything would have been made in the most perfect way possible. That is why I thought that he who wanted to explain why things came to be, perished or subsisted had to search for what suited the perfection of each. Thus man would only have to consider in himself or in some other thing, what was best or most perfect, alone. For he who knew the most perfect would easily decide thereby what was imperfect, since there is only one true knowledge of both.

'In view of all this, I rejoiced to have found a master able to teach the reason of things: whether, for example, the earth was round or flat, and why it was best that way rather than otherwise ... Moreover, I expected that when he said that the earth was or was not at the centre of the universe, he would explain to me why that was the most suitable. And when he said the same of the sun, the moon, the stars and their motions ... And finally, after showing what was suitable to each thing individually, he would show me what was best in general.

'Full of this hope, I took and skimmed through the books of Anaxagoras with great eagerness, but I was far from my expectation, for I was surprised to see that he made no use of this governing Intelligence', set out in advance, 'that he spoke no more of the adornment and the perfection of things, and introduced some rather implausible ethereal matters.

'In this, he was rather like the man who said that Socrates did things intelligently, but when he came to explaining in particular the causes of his actions, thereupon said that he was sitting here because he had a body composed of bone, flesh and nerves, that the bones were solid, but had gaps and joints, that the nerves could be tensed or relaxed, and that was why the body was flexible and I was sitting. Or if he wanted to explain the present speech, he had recourse to the air, to vocal and aural organs and like things, while forgetting the true causes, that is that the Athenians thought it better to condemn than to acquit me, and I for my part thought it better to sit here than to take flight. For, by my faith, these nerves and these bones would long since be with the Boeotians and the Megarans, if I had not found it more just and more honest for me to suffer the penalty the fatherland wants to impose on me than live elsewhere a wanderer in exile. That is why it is unreasonable to call these bones and nerves and their motions causes.

'It is true that whoever said that I could not do all this without bones and nerves would be right, but the true cause is something else ... and that is no more than a condition without which the cause could not be the cause ...

'People who say no more than, for example, that the motions of the bodies surrounding the earth support the earth where it is, forget that the divine power arranges everything in the finest way, and do not understand that it is the good and the beautiful that join, form and preserve the world ...' Thus far Socrates, for the things about ideas or forms that follow in Plato are not less excellent but a bit more difficult.

21. If the rules of mechanics depended on Geometry alone without Metaphysics, the phenomena would be quite different

Now, since the wisdom of God has always been recognised in the details of the +mechanical+ structures of particular bodies, it is very necessary that it should also be shown in the general set-up of the world and the constitution of the laws of nature. This is so true that the counsels of this Wisdom are observed in the laws of motion in general. For if there were nothing else to bodies but an extended mass and nothing to motion but change of place, and if everything had to and could be deduced from these definitions +alone by geometrical necessity+, it would follow, as I have shown elsewhere,[23] that the least body would give the same speed as its own to the largest resting body it met without losing any of its own, and many other rules of this sort would have to be accepted, such as are altogether contrary to the construction of a system. But the decree of the divine wisdom to preserve always the same total force and direction has provided for this.

I even find that many natural effects can be demonstrated doubly, i.e. through the *efficient cause and separately through the *final cause as well, by using for example the decree of God to produce His effect by the +simplest and most determinate ways+, as I have shown elsewhere[24] in my account of the rules of *catoptrics and *dioptrics+, and I shall say more of it below[25]+.

22. Reconciliation of the two ways by *final and *efficient causes ⟨in defence of⟩[a] both those who explain nature *mechanically and those who have recourse to incorporeal natures

It is good to note this point to reconcile those who hope to explain *mechanically the formation of the first tissues of an animal and the complete machine of its parts with those who account for the same structure by *final causes. Both are good and both can be useful, not only for admiring the artifice of the great Workman, but also in discovering something useful in physics and medicine. Authors who follow these different routes should not be hard on each other.

For I see that those who concentrate on explaining the beauty of divine Anatomy laugh at others who imagine that an +apparently fortuitous+ motion of particular fluids can make such a beautiful variety of members, and call such people rash and profane, while on the other hand the latter call the former simple and superstitious like the ancients who took it that the physicists were impious when they held that it was not Jupiter that thundered but some matter in the clouds. The best thing would be to unite both considerations, for, to use a vulgar comparison, the skill of a workman is recognised and praised not only by showing what designs he had when he made the parts of his machine, but also by explaining the tools he used to make each part, particularly when these tools are simple and ingeniously contrived. *God is skilful enough an artisan* to produce a machine a thousand times still more ingenious than that of our body [if that were possible], using only a few simple enough fluids expressly formed so that only the ordinary laws of nature are needed to sort them out as necessary to produce such an admirable effect, but it is also true that this would not happen if God were not the Author of nature.

I find, nevertheless, that the way of *efficient causes is +while indeed more profound and in one way more direct and *a priori*, on the other hand+ rather difficult when we get down to details and I think that our Philosophers are most often still rather far from that. In contrast, the way of *final causes is easier and is moreover often helpful in guessing important +and useful+ truths that would have been a long time in the searching by the former +more physical+ route, and of this Anatomy can furnish important examples. I also hold that Snell[26], the first discoverer of the rules of refraction, would have taken a long time to find them if he had tried to find out first how light was formed. But he seems to have followed the method the ancients used in *catoptrics, that of *final causes in fact. For, in the search for the easiest way of conducting a ray from one given point to another by reflection at a given plane,+ (supposing that this is nature's design), +they discovered the equality of the angles of incidence and reflection+, as can be seen in a little treatise of Heliodorus of Larissa[27] and elsewhere+. That is what in my opinion Snell, and after him (though without knowing anything about him) Fermat[28], applied more ingeniously to refraction. For when +in the same media +the rays observe the same proportion of sines+ which is also that of the resistances of the media+, it turns out to be the easiest, or at least the most determinate way of passing from a given point in one medium to a given point in the other. The demonstration Descartes tried to give of this same theorem +by the way of *efficient causes+ is far from being as good. At least there are grounds for suspecting that he would never have found it that way if he had not heard something of Snell's discovery in Holland.

a.   Amended in MS to 'in answer to'.

23.   Returning to immaterial substances; the explanation of how God acts on the understanding of minds and of whether we always have an idea of what we think

I have found it relevant to insist somewhat on these considerations concerning final causes +, incorporeal natures and an Intelligent Cause in relation to bodies,+ to make known their use even in

physics and mathematics. On the one hand, this is to purge the
*mechanical philosophy of the profanity imputed to it. On the
other hand it is to raise the minds of our philosophers from mere
material considerations to more noble meditations. It is now time
to return from bodies to immaterial natures, to minds in particular,
and to say something of the ways God uses to illumine them and
act on them, for we must not doubt that here¶ too there are laws
of nature, a point I could discuss more fully elsewhere. For now, it
is enough to touch a little on ideas, on whether we see all things in
God, and on how God is our light.

Now, it is relevant to note that several errors are occasioned by
the misuse of ideas. For when we reason on something we imagine
we have an idea of it, and on that foundation some[29] ⟨recent
authors⟩[a] have built a demonstration of God that is[, rigorously
speaking,] very imperfect. For, they[29] say, I must have an idea of
God or of a perfect being, since I am thinking of Him, and it is
impossible to think without an idea. +Now the idea of this Being
includes all the perfections and existence is one of these, so that
consequently He exists. +But as we often think of impossible
chimerae, such as the ultimate degree of speed or the greatest
number or the meeting of the chonchoid with its base or rule, this
reasoning is not enough. Hence in this sense a person can say he
has true or false ideas according as the thing in question is possible
or not, and it is only when we are assured of its possibility that we
can boast of having an idea of the thing. Thus the above argument
proves at least that God necessarily exists if He is possible. This is
indeed an excellent privilege of the divine nature: to need only its
possibility or essence to exist in fact, just what is called an *Ens a se.

a.   Amended in MS to 'ancient and modern philosophers'.

24.   Just what is clear or obscure, distinct or confused, adequate and intuitive or suppositive knowledge, and what are nominal, real, causal and essential definitions[30]

The better to understand the nature of ideas, we have to touch a
little on the varieties of knowledge. [When I know only through
experience that something is possible, because everything that
exists is possible, my knowledge is confused. It is in this way that

¶.   Reading *où* for *ou*.

we know bodies and their qualities. But when I can prove *a priori* that something is possible, this knowledge is distinct.] When I can recognise one thing among others without being able to say in what its **differentiae* or properties consist, my knowledge is *confused*. Thus it is that we sometimes know *clearly* without being in any doubt at all whether a poem or picture is well or badly made, because there is an I don't know what that satisfies or shocks us. But only when I can explain the marks available to me is my knowledge called *distinct*. Such is the knowledge of the assayer who discerns the true and the false by particular tests or marks comprising the definition of gold.

But there are degrees of distinct knowledge, for the notions that enter the definition would ordinarily themselves need definition and are only confusedly known. But when every thing that enters a definition or distinct item of knowledge is distinctly known right back to the primitive notions, I call this knowledge *adequate*, and when my mind understands all the primitive ingredients of a notion¶ all at once and distinctly, then it has an intuitive knowledge of it, something very rare since most human knowledge is confused or even *suppositive*.

It is also good to distinguish nominal definitions from real ones. I refer to a nominal definition when it is still possible to doubt that the notion defined is possible. Thus, for example, when I say that an endless screw is a solid line whose parts are congruent or can coincide with each other, whoever did not otherwise know what an endless screw was could doubt the possibility of such a line, though indeed it was a reciprocal property of an endless screw, since the other lines whose parts are congruent are planar (the circumference of the circle and the straight line only), that is they can be drawn *in a plane*. This shows that every reciprocal property can be used in a nominal definition, whereas when the property makes known the possibility of the thing, it makes the definition real. +As long as we have a mere nominal definition, we could never be sure of the consequences drawn from it, for if it concealed some contradiction or impossibility, contrary conclusions could be drawn from it. That is why truths do not depend on names and are not arbitrary as held by some new philosophers.+[31]

¶. Marginal note by Leibniz: '*N.B.* A notion is intermediate between intuitive and clear when I have a clear knowledge of every notion that prevents me from being deceived.'

For the rest, there remains a considerable difference between the kinds of real definition. When possibility is only proved by experience, as in the definition of quicksilver +whose possibility is known because we know that such a body, a very heavy but rather volatile fluid, actually exists+, the definition is then merely real and nothing more. When one the other hand the proof of possibility is done *a priori*, the definition is real and causal as well+, as when it incorporates the possibility of generating the thing+. When it takes the analysis to the limit as far as the primitive notions, supposing nothing in need of *a priori* proof of its possibility, the definition is perfect or *essential*.

25. In what case our knowledge is joined to the contemplation of the idea

Now it is obvious that we have no idea of a notion when it is impossible. And when our knowledge is merely *suppositive*, when we have the idea we do not contemplate it, for such a notion is known only in the same way as those that are occultly impossible+, and if it is possible it is not learned by that method of knowing+. For example, when I think of a thousand+, or of chiliagon+, I [often] do so without contemplating the idea, as when I say that a thousand is ten times a hundred without putting myself to the trouble of thinking what ten and a hundred are. That is because *I suppose* I know it and see no need for the present to pause to conceive it. Thus it can easily happen, as indeed it +does often enough+, that I am in error with respect to a notion I suppose or believe I understand, although in truth it is impossible +, or at least incompatible with the others I join it to+. Whether or not I am in error, this suppositive way of conceiving remains the same. Hence, it is only when our knowledge of confused things is *clear* or our knowledge of distinct things intuitive, that we ⟨contemplate⟩ᵃ the complete idea of them.

a.   Revised in MS to 'see'.

26.   We have all ideas in us; Plato's notion of reminiscence

If we are to conceive properly what an idea is, we must avoid an ambiguity. For there are some[32] who take the idea to be the form or way of distinguishing our thoughts. On this view we have the idea in our minds only to the extent that we think of it+, and whenever we think of it again, we have ideas of the same thing different from though similar to the previous ones+. But it seems that others[33] take the idea to be an immediate object of thought, or some permanent form remaining when we do not contemplate it. Indeed, there is always in our souls the capacity to conceive any nature or form whatever, when the opportunity of thinking of it presents itself. I think that this capacity of our souls, to the extent that it expresses some nature, form or essence, is properly speaking the idea of the thing, in us and always in us, whether we think of it or not. For our soul expresses God and the universe, and all essences as well as all existences.

This ⟨follows from⟩[a] my principles, for nothing enters our minds naturally from outside, and it is a bad habit of ours to think as if our souls received some messenger* species or had gates and windows. We have all the forms in our minds, for all time even, because the mind always expresses all its future thoughts, and already thinks confusedly everything it will ever think distinctly. Nothing could be taught us whose idea was not already present in our minds as the matter from which this thought was formed.

That is what Plato understood so well when he put forward his doctrine of reminiscence, which is very sound provided we take it the right way and purge it of the error of pre-existence+, and do not imagine that the soul has to have once known and distinctly thought what it is now learning and thinking+. He also confirmed his opinion by a beautiful experiment. He introduced a little boy [in his dialogue called *Meno*] whom he led insensibly into the most difficult geometrical truths concerning incommensurables, without teaching him anything, merely putting relevant questions in order. This shows that our souls +have virtual knowledge of everything. They +need only attention to know the truths, and consequently have at least the truths on which these truths depend. It can even be said, if the latter are taken for the relations of ideas, that they already possess these truths.

[a]amended in MS to 'agrees with'.

27. ⟨In what sense⟩[a] our souls may be compared to empty tablets, and how our notions come from the senses

Aristotle preferred to compare our souls to tablets that were still bare with space for writing on+, and he claimed that nothing was in our understanding that did not come from the senses+.[34] As is the way with Aristotle, this is more in conformity with popular notions, whereas Plato goes deeper. Nevertheless, such everyday expressions or practical sayings are liable to pass into common usage, almost as with the followers of Copernicus who continue to say that the sun rises and sets. I often find, even, that a good sense can be given to them in accordance with which there is nothing wrong with them. Just as I have already remarked on the way it is possible to say truly that particular substances act on each other, in this same sense it can be said that we receive some knowledge from outside by the ministry of the senses, because some external things contain, or more particularly express, the reasons determining our souls to particular thoughts. But when we are concerned with the accuracy of metaphysical truths, it is important to recognise the *extent and independence of our souls. This goes infinitely further than is vulgarly supposed, although in the ordinary course of life only what is more certainly perceived and belongs to us in a particular way is attributed to it, since there is no purpose in going further.

Nevertheless, it would be good to choose special terms for both senses to avoid ambiguity. Hence, expressions in our souls, whether conceived or not, can be called *ideas*, while those we conceive or form can be called *notions* or *concepts*. But however we take it, it is always false to say that all our notions come from the senses called external, since the one I have of myself, and of my thoughts, and consequently of being, substance, action, identity and many others, comes from internal experience.

a.   Revised in MS to 'How'.

28.   God alone is the immediate object of our perceptions existing outside us, ⟨for⟩[a] He alone is our light

Now, in the rigour of metaphysical truth, there is no external cause acting on us but God alone, and He alone communicates himself to us directly in virtue of our continual dependence. It follows from this that there is no other external object touching our souls+ and exciting our perceptions directly+. So it is only in virtue of the continual action of God on us that we have in our souls the ideas of everything , i.e. because every effect expresses its cause and hence the essence of our souls is a particular expression, imitation, or image of the essence, thought and will of God and of all the ideas included in Him. Hence, it can be said that God alone is our immediate object outside us, and that it is ⟨in⟩[b] Him that we see all things. For example, when we see the sun and the stars, it is God who gave us them and preserves their ideas in us, and in fact determines us to think of them at the time at which our senses are disposed in a particular way, +through His ordinary *concurrence and +in accordance with the laws established by Him. God is the sun and light of souls, 'the light enlightening every man born into the world'.[35] It is not just today that people are of this opinion. After Holy Scripture and the Fathers — always more for Plato than for Aristotle — I recall noticing once that in the time of the *Scholastics some believed that God was the light of the soul and, in their way of speaking, 'the *active intellect of the rational soul'.[36] The *Averroists gave this a bad meaning, but others such as, I think, William of St Amour[37] [doctor of the Sorbonne] and several mystical theologians, took it in a manner worthy of God and capable of raising the soul to the knowledge of its good.

a. Amended in MS to 'and'.

b. Amended in MS to 'by'.

29. Nevertheless we think+ directly+ by our own ideas and not by those of God

Nevertheless I am not of the opinion of some able philosophers[38] who +seem to+ maintain that our very ideas are in God, and not at all in us. In my opinion, this comes about because they have still not pondered enough +what we have just explained concerning substances, nor +the entire *extent and independence of our souls (which means that they include everything happening to them and *express [the essence of] God, +and with Him all possible and actual beings,+ like an effect its cause). Also, it is inconceivable that I should think by means of the thoughts of someone else. It is [very necessary that an effect should express its cause and it is] also very necessary that the soul should be actually affected in a particular way when it thinks of something and that it should have in advance, not only the passive power of being affected in this way, something already determined, but also an active power, in virtue of which there has always been in its nature the marks of the future production of that thought and dispositions to produce it when the time came. +All this already includes the idea contained in that thought.+

30. **How God inclines without necessitating; we have no right to complain, and we must not ask why[a] Judas sins [+since this free action is included in his notion+], only why Judas the sinner is admitted to existence in preference to other possible persons. [+The origin of evil comes from this+] +The original imperfection before sin, and the degrees of grace+**

Concerning the action of God on the human will, there are many rather difficult questions that would take time to pursue here. Nevertheless, in outline,[b] this is what can be said. When God *concurs in our actions, He ordinarily does no more than follow the laws [of nature] He has established, i.e. He preserves and continually produces our ⟨nature⟩,[c] so that the thoughts +spontaneously [and naturally] or freely+ happen to us in the order carried by the notion of our individual substance+, within which they could have been foreseen from all eternity+. Moreover, in virtue of the decree that the will should always tend towards the +apparent+ good+, and so express or imitate God's will in certain particular respects in respect of which this apparent good always has something of the true+, He determines our will to choose what seems the best without nonetheless necessitating it. For, absolutely speaking, +in so far as it may be opposed to necessity,+ our will is indifferent +and has the power to do otherwise or to suspend its action altogether,+ since both are and remain possible.

Hence it falls to the soul to take precautions against the appearances taking it by surprise by means of a firm resolve to reflect and to refuse to act or judge on particular occasions without thorough deliberation. Nevertheless it is true and even certain from all eternity that a particular soul will not use this power on one such occasion. But who could do anything about it or do other than complain about himself? For all complaints after the fact are unjust when they would have been unjust before. Now would this soul, shortly before sinning, be in the right to complain of God, [who has not determined him to flee from the sin] as if He had determined him to sin? Since God's determinations in these matters are unforeseeable, how does he know himself to be determined to sin, unless in fact he is already actually sinning? It is only a matter of not willing, and God could propose no easier +or juster+ condition. +Moreover, any judge stops only to consider how far a man's will is bad without searching for the reasons disposing him to have a bad will.+ But perhaps it is certain from all eternity that I will sin? Answer yourself: perhaps not. Do not think about what you cannot know and cannot enlighten you, but act in accordance with the duty you know.

But, someone else will ask, whence comes it that that man will certainly do this sin? The answer is easy: otherwise he would not be that man. For God sees for all time that there will be a certain Judas whose notion, or idea God has of him, contains this future free action. Hence the only question that remains is why such a Judas, the traitor, who is merely a possible in the idea of God, actually exists. But to that question there is no answer to be expected here below, unless that in general we must say that since God thought it good for him to exist, despite the sin he foresaw, this evil must be repaid with interest in the universe; +that God will obtain a greater good from it;+ and that in all He will find this sequence of things +including the existence of this sinner+ the most perfect of all the other possible ones. But to explain in all cases the admirable economy of this choice is not possible while we are travellers [in this vale of tears] in this world. It is enough to know without understanding it. It is time here to recognise 'the height of the riches',[39] the width and depth of the divine wisdom, without seeking a detail involving these infinite considerations.

Nevertheless, it is clear that God is not the cause of evil. For not only did original sin take hold of the soul after the loss of innocence but before then there was a limitation or original imperfection common to the natures of all creatures +making them capable of sin or liable to fail+. Thus there is no more difficulty with regard to the *supralapsarians than with the others. In my opinion, it is to this that the opinion of St Augustine and other authors that the root of evil is in nothingness should be reduced, i.e. in the privation or the limitation of creatures that God graciously remedies by giving them the degree of pefection it pleases Him to give.+ Whether ordinary or extraordinary, this grace of God has its degrees and measures, always in itself efficacious in producing a proportionate effect. Moreover it is always sufficient, not only to guarantee us against sin, but to produce salvation, if the man joins himself to it with ⟨his will⟩,ᵈ though it is not always sufficient to surmount human inclinations, otherwise it would depend on nothing more, and that is reserved to the absolutely efficacious grace alone that is always victorious +whether by itself or by the congruity of circumstances+.

a.   Here Leibniz originally wrote: 'if Judas had not sinned he would not be who he is.'

b.   Originally here Leibniz contemplated expounding a distinction between indifferent, good and bad actions but dropped the issue in drafting.

c.   Revised in MS to read 'being'.

d.   Amended in MS to 'what is in him'.

31.ᵃ   +[The foreknowledge of merit, the dispensing of grace], the motives of election, the *middle knowledge, the absolute decree; that everything reduces to the reason why God chose a particular possible person for existence, whose notion includes that particular sequence of graces +and free actions, so that all the difficulties are removed at once+

In the end, the graces of God are graces pure and simple over which creatures have no claim. ᵇ+However, just as when we are giving an account of the action of God in dispensing these graces it is not enough to have recourse to His foresight, whether absolute or conditional, of the future actions of men, so we must not imagine absolute decrees with no reasonable motive. As regards God's foresight of faith and good works, it is very true that God has elected only those whose faith and charity He foresaw, 'those He foreknew He would give faith to',⁴⁰ but the same question returns: why God will give the grace of faith and good works to some rather than to others. As for this [middle] knowledge of God's, the foresight, not of good works, but of their matter and predisposition, or of what the man would contribute from his side

+(since it is true that there is diversity on the human side wherever there is on the side of grace, and since indeed, although man needs to be excited towards the good and converted, it is very necessary that he should also play his part here after the fact)+ some people think that it could be said that since God sees what man would do without grace or extraordinary assistance, or at least what he will have on his side apart from grace, He could resolve to give grace to those whose natural disposition was the best or at any rate the least imperfect or least evil. But if that was the case, it could be said that these natural dispositions+, in so far as they are good+, are still the effect of an act of grace, even if an ordinary one, since God has advantaged some more than others. And since He well knows that these natural advantages He gives will provide the motive for grace or extraordinary assistance, does it not follow from the doctrine that truly everything in the end reduces to His mercy?

Hence, I believe +(since we do not know how much or how God takes account of natural dispositions in dispensing grace)+ that the most accurate and certain thing to say is+, as already noted and in conformity with our principles,+ that among the possible beings there should be the person of Peter or John whose notion or idea contains the whole sequence of ordinary and extraordinary graces and all the other events along with their circumstances, and that it pleased God to choose him from among an infinity of other equally possible persons for actual existence. After that it seems that there is no more to ask and that all the difficulties disappear.

For, considering this single great question, why it pleased God to choose one from so many other possible persons, we would have to be unreasonable indeed not to be satisfied with the general reasons given, for which the detail is beyond our reach. So, we should not have recourse to an absolute decree, which is unreasonable since there is no reason for it, or to reasons that do not succeed in resolving the difficulty. Instead the best will be to say with St Paul[b]+ that there are certain grand reasons for this +unknown to mortals+ and founded in the general order whose aim is the greatest perfection of the universe, and that God has observed these. It is to this that the motives of the glory of God and the manifestation of His justice reduce, as well as His mercy and His perfections generally+, and finally that immense depth of His riches Paul's soul was enchanted with+.

a. This entire section was added in MS by Leibniz.

b. Entire passage added in MS.

32. Usefulness of these principles in matters of piety and religion

For the rest, it seems that the thoughts we have just explained+, particularly the grand principle of the perfection of the operations of God and the notion of the substance including all the events with all their circumstances+, far from harming religion, serve to confirm it, removing very great difficulties, inflaming souls with a divine love and raising minds to the knowledge of incorporeal substances to a much greater extent than the hypotheses we have seen up to now. For it is clear that just as thoughts ⟨depend on⟩[a] our substance, all other substances depend on God, that God is all in all, and that He is intimately united with all creatures +(though to the extent of their perfection)+, and that He alone determines them externally by His influence. And if to act is to determine directly, it can be said in this sense, +in the language of metaphysics, +that God operates on me and is alone able to do me good or ill+, while other substances ⟨are nothing but *occasional causes⟩,[b]+ for the reason that as God considers all of them, He distributes His acts of goodness and obliges them to conform to each other. Also, God alone makes the connection and communication of substances, and it is by Him that phenomena of any given substance meet and fit with those of the others, and consequently that there is reality in our perceptions. But in practice action is attributed to particular ⟨*occasional causes⟩[c] in the sense explained above,[41] because it is not always necessary to mention the universal cause in particular cases.

It is seen also that every substance has a perfect spontaneity (which in intelligent substances becomes liberty): that everything that happens to it is a consequence of its ideas or being, and that it is determined by nothing but God alone. That is why a person of noble mind whose sanctity is greatly revered used to say that the soul must often think as if there were only God and it in the world.[42]

Now nothing makes immortality more completely comprehensible than this independence and *extent of the soul. It protects it absolutely from all external things, since it alone constitutes the whole world and, with God, suffices to itself. It is also impossible for it to perish other than by annihilation, and impossible for the world (of which it is a living and perpetual *expression) to destroy itself. Hence, it is not possible for the changes in that extended mass called our body to do anything to our soul, or for the disappearance of that body to destroy what is indivisible.

a. Amended in MS to '*emanate from'.

b. Later changed to 'only contribute by reason of these determinations'.

c. Later changed to 'reasons'.

33.ᵃ Explanation of the union of soul and body +something once thought inexplicable or miraculous, and the origin of confused perceptions+

Also clear is the unexpected solution of that great mystery of the union of soul and body, i.e. how it happens that the actions and *passions of the one are accompanied by the actions and passions+, or rather appropriate *phenomena+, of the other. For there is no way of conceiving any influence of the one on the other, and it is unreasonable simply to have recourse +to the extraordinary operation of +the universal cause+ in something ordinary and particular+. But here is the true reason. ᵇ⟨We have said that everything happening to the soul and to every substance is a consequence of its notion. +Hence the very idea or essence of the soul makes all its appearances or perceptions+ arise spontaneously out of its own nature, and just so, that they answer of themselves to what happens⟩ in the whole universe, though particularly in the body assigned to it, +because in a way and for a time,+ it is in accordance with the relation of other bodies to its own that the soul expresses the state of the universe. +This shows yet again how our bodies belong to us without nevertheless being attached to our *essences. I believe that persons able to meditate will see advantage in our principles in just this, that it is easy to see in what exactly the connection between soul and body — apparently inexplicable by any other means — consists.

+It can also be seen that the perceptions of our senses, even when they are clear, must necessarily contain some confused sensations. For as all the bodies in the universe are in sympathy, ours receive the impressions of all the others. Although our senses relate to everything, it is not possible for our souls to attend to all individually, and that is why our confused sensations are the result of a variety, altogether infinite, of perceptions. It is almost like the confused murmur heard by those approaching the shores of the sea that arises from the accumulation of the reverberations of innumerable waves. Now if of several perceptions (not coming together to become a single one) none stands out above the others, and if they make almost equally strong impressions, or are equally capable of determining the attention of the soul, it can only register them confusedly.+

a.   Initially, the material of this section formed part of the previous one.

b.   This initially read: ':since every substance expresses the whole universe, the actions or passions of the soul which the very idea or essence guides, respond of themselves to what happens in the body and even ...'

34.   ⟨The excellence of minds compared with⟩ᵃ other substances or *substantial forms. +The immortality called for implies memory+

[One thing I do not propose to decide is whether in metaphysical rigour bodies are substances or are no more than *true* phenomena like the rainbow, nor consequently whether there are substances, souls or substantial forms that are not intelligent. But] if we suppose that bodies like man that constitute unities in themselves are substances and have *substantial forms, we are obliged to admit that these souls and substantial forms could no more entirely perish than atoms [if there are any] or ultimate particles of matter can, in the opinion of other philosophers. For though it may become quite different, no substance perishes. Although more imperfectly than minds, they too express the whole universe. But the principal difference is that they do not know what they are +nor what they are doing. Consequently, since they have no power of reflection, they are unable to discover necessary and universal truths. It is also for want of reflection on themselves that they have no moral qualities,+ so that, when we consider how a caterpillar changes into a butterfly through almost a thousand transformations, it comes to the same for morals and practice as saying that they perish, as can indeed be said physically +(as we say of bodies that they perish by corruption)+. But the intelligent soul that knows what it is, and is capable of pronouncing this *me* which says so much, not only ⟨remains the same⟩[b] metaphysically +to a greater extent than the others+, but it also remains morally the same and constitutes the same personality. For it is the memory and knowledge of this *me* that makes it liable to punishment and reward. Also, the immortality called for +both in morality and religion+ does not consist merely in that perpetual subsistence proper to all substances. For without the memory of what has been, there would be nothing desirable about it. Let us suppose that some ⟨poor wretch⟩[c] suddenly became King of China, but only on condition that he forgot what he had been+, as if he had just been reborn+: does that not come to the same in practice+, or in the effects that could be registered,+ as if he had to be annihilated and a King of China created at the same instant and at the same place? Something this individual has no reason to desire.

a.   Revised in MS to read: 'The difference between minds and . . .'.

b.   Revised in MS to 'and subsists'.

c.   Revised in MS to 'individual'.

35. The excellence of minds. God considers them in preference to other creatures. +Minds express God rather than the world, but other substances express the world rather than God+

But to show by natural reasons that God always will preserve not only our substance but also our personality, that is memory and knowledge of what we are +although distinct knowledge of that may sometimes by suspended when asleep or unconscious+, morality must be joined to Metaphysics. That is, God has not only to be considered as the principle and cause of all substances +and all beings+, but also as the chief of all persons +or intelligent substances+ and the absolute monarch of the most perfect city or republic, like that of the universe +composed of all minds together+, since God himself is the most accomplished of all

Minds as well as the greatest of all Beings. For assuredly, minds are ⟨either the only substances existing in the world if bodies are no more than true phenomena, or else they are at least the most perfect ones⟩.ᵃ And since the whole nature, end, virtue and function of substances is merely to *express God and the universe, as has been sufficiently explained,⁴³ there are no grounds for doubting that substances expressing Him in the knowledge of what they are doing, and capable of knowing great truths regarding God and the universe, express Him incomparably better than those natures that are either animal and incapable of knowing truths, or altogether destitute of sense and knowledge; and the difference +between intelligent substances and those that are not+ is as great as that between the mirror and he who sees.

And since God Himself is the greatest and wisest of minds, it is easy to conclude that beings with whom He can so to speak enter into conversation or even into fellowship, communicating His thoughts and intentions individually, so that they can know and love their Benefactor, must concern Him infinitely more than all other beings, able only to pass for the tools of minds, just as we can see wise persons taking infinitely more account of a man than of some other thing, however precious that may be. It seems that the greatest satisfaction an otherwise contented soul can have is to see himself loved by others +although in respect of God there is this difference that His glory and our worship can add nothing to His satisfaction, since the knowledge of creatures is no more than a consequence of His sovereign and perfect happiness and very far from contributing to the latter or being part of the cause thereof.+ Nevertheless, what is good and reasonable in finite minds is supremely so in Him and just as we would praise a king who preferred to preserve the life of a man before the most precious and rare of animals, we should not doubt that the most enlightened and just of all Monarchs is of the same opinion.

a. Revised in MS to read 'the most perfect beings and best express the Godhead'.

36. God is the monarch of that most perfect republic that consists of all minds, and the happiness of this city of God is His principal design

In fact, minds are the most perfectible of all substances and their perfections have this characteristic that they hinder each other the least+, or rather that they assist each other, for only the most virtuous can be the most perfect friends+. Hence it manifestly follows that God who always looks to the greatest perfection in general, will have the most care of minds, and will give them, not only generally but to each individually, the greatest perfection the universal harmony can permit.

+It can even be said that God, in so far as He is+ a mind+, is the origin of existent things — if there were no will to choose best there would be no reason for one possible thing to exist in preference to others. Hence God's quality of being Himself a mind precedes all other considerations He may have with respect to creatures.[a] ⟨Minds only are made in His image, and it is as if they are of His race and children of His house, since they alone can serve Him freely and act consciously in imitation of the divine nature. One mind is worth an entire world, since it does not only *express it, but knows it, and governs itself there in the manner of God. So much so that it seems that while every substance expresses the whole universe, other substances *express the world rather than God while minds express God rather than the world. And this natural nobility of minds, which brings them as near to the divine as is possible for mere creatures, means that God receives from them infinitely more glory than from other beings, or rather other beings merely give minds matter for glorifying Him.⟩

That is why this moral quality of God that makes Him the Lord and Monarch of Minds, affects Him so to speak personally in a quite special manner. It is in this that He becomes human and is willing to allow human ways of speaking about Him, and enters into fellowship with us like a Prince with his subjects. This consideration is so dear to Him that the happy and flourishing state of His empire, that consists in the greatest possible happiness of the inhabitants, becomes ⟨the supreme *subaltern law of His conduct⟩.[b] For happiness is to persons what perfection is to beings, and if the first principle of existence of the physical world is the decree giving it the greatest possible perfection, the first ⟨principle of existence⟩[c] of the moral world or City of God, the most noble part of the universe, must be to spread as much happiness as possible in it.

Hence it must not be doubted that God so ordained (+not only+ that minds could live forever, +which is inevitable, but also that they should conserve forever their moral nature,+) so that this city should lose no person just as the world loses no substance. And consequently, they will always know what they are, otherwise they would not be liable to reward or punishment, which however is the essence of any republic+, above all of one that is the most perfect, in which nothing can be neglected+.

Finally, since God is at once the most just and the most good-natured of monarchs, and asks only for good will, provided that it is sincere and serious, His subjects could not hope for better conditions: to make them perfectly happy, He wants only that they love Him.

a.   Section subject to extensive reworkings and additions in MS.

b.   Revised in MS to read 'his supreme law'.

c.   Revised in MS to read 'object'.

37.   Jesus Christ has revealed to men the mystery and admirable laws of the Kingdom of Heaven and the greatness of the supreme happiness God prepares for those who love Him

The ancient philosophers had very little knowledge of these important truths. Jesus Christ alone expressed them divinely well and in such a clear and familiar way, that the most crude minds came to understand them.[44] So His gospel changed the entire face of human affairs. He brought us knowledge of +the Kingdom of Heaven or this perfect republic of minds that merits the title 'City of God' whose admirable laws he revealed to us, and he alone shows us+ how much God loves us; the exactness with which He has provided for all that concerns us; that since He cares for sparrows, He will not neglect the reasonable creatures who are infinitely more dear to Him; +that all the hairs in our heads are counted; +that heaven and earth will pass away before the Word of God and everything belonging to the pattern of our salvation is changed; God has more concern with the least of intelligent souls than with the whole machine of the world; that we must not fear those who can destroy the body but are unable to harm souls, since God alone can make them happy or unhappy; that the just are in His hand protected from all the revolutions of the universe,

+since nothing can act on them but God alone+; that none of our actions is forgotten; that everything is taken into account, right down to unguarded words, and a spoonful of water well used; and finally that all things must result in the greatest good for those that are good; that the just are like suns and that neither our senses nor our minds have ever tasted anything approaching the happiness God prepares for those who love Him.

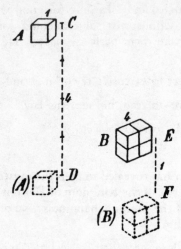

from G iv, 443

Notes on text of *Discourse*

1 Leibniz has, amongst others, Descartes in mind. See *Supp.* 3 and 9.

2 The reference is to talk of God *looking at* the world in Genesis, for instance in this verse: 'And God saw what he had made, and it was very good'. (*New English Bible*, Genesis 1, v. 31). Our phrase 'anthropomorphic way of speaking' corresponds to Leibniz's 'anthropologie'.

3 It is possible that Leibniz had in mind the Appendix to Part One of Spinoza's *Ethics*, on which he had written notes in 1678. (See PPL 205, G i 150) Spinoza there attacks the way in which men imagine God to be possessed of human qualities:

> ... there are men lunatic enough to believe, that even God himself takes pleasure in harmony; and philosophers are not lacking who have persuaded themselves, that the motion of the heavenly bodies gives rise to harmony — all of which instances sufficiently show that everyone judges of things according to the state of his brain, or rather mistakes for things the forms of his imagination. (*Spinoza: On the Improvement of the Understanding* etc., trans. RHM Elwes, New York, 1955, p. 80)

4 See *Supp.* 3 for the relevance of these remarks to the earlier criticism of Descartes.

5 For a discussion of Descartes's voluntarism and its implications for his account of eternal truths, see Osler (1985).

6 Leibniz quotes a Latin source at this point: '*Uti minus malum habet rationem boni, ita minus bonum habet rationem mali*'.

7 Leibniz quotes a Latin source at this point: '*Idem velle et idem nolle amicitia est*'.

8 Geomancy was a form of divination in which shapes and lines are randomly produced, by throwing each or, as with the case Leibniz has in mind, by putting dots on a piece of paper. The supposed art of reading tea leaves may descend from geomancy. This and other 'occult sciences' were defended in the seventeenth century by writers such as Robert Fludd in his *Mosaic Philosophy*, to whom Leibniz made occasional reference (see *Supp.* 6 and 14 below).

9 This is a distinction drawn by Malebranche. It is explained by Leibniz in *Supp.* 5.

10   The reference is clearly to Malebranche and the *occasionalists who held that God is the only true cause and that what are ordinarily thought of as causes are no more than occasions on which God regularly acts. See *Supp.* 6.

11   The reference is to Descartes in particular, whose view that God conserves the total quantity of motion in the universe is criticised in §17.

12   Leibniz here cites the Scholastic maxim *actiones sunt suppositorum*.

13   Literally 'thisness', an allusion to the theory of what makes something an individual substance produced by Duns Scotus and in which Leibniz had taken an interest when writing a student dissertation. Every individual has its own *haecceity*, according to Duns Scotus, though (like Leibniz) he believed it was only known to God.

14   The quotation *quod ibi omne individuum sit species infima* is from Aquinas. See *Summa Theologica*, Question 50, Article 4.

15   In the *Discourse* Leibniz is making the conscious supposition that bodies are substances, indicating at several points (e.g. §§9 and 34) that he is only assuming that they are. If they are, they must, be argues, be real unities — a true substance must be an *unum per se*. That bodies are substances was denied by Plato and, following him, by Augustine, according to Leibniz (see, for instance, G ii 118). Leibniz was convinced by Arnauld that he could not maintain that material bodies were substances in a strict sense. By 1690 Leibniz had fully conceded this point in writing to Arnauld: 'A body is an aggregation of substances, and is not a substance, properly speaking' (G ii 135). In *Supps.* 7 and 19 Leibniz seems on his way to this conclusion.

16   Leibniz thought it was going beyond reasonable bounds to offer explanations in terms of a first cause as if these were rivals to explanations in terms of ordinary ('secondary') causes. His own view was that 'there is no natural truth in things for which we must find the reason in the divine action or will but that God has always put into things themselves properties by which all their predicates can be explained' (PPL 441).

17   Leibniz thought that the Cartesians were unreasonable in their belief that animals had no souls. As against Descartes he elsewhere objected that 'to ascribe a substantial form and perception, or a soul, to man alone is as ridiculous as to believe that everything has been made for man alone and that the earth is the centre of the universe' (PPL 289). This objection is a metaphysical one, turning on the perfection of God and the consequential richness of the universe.

18   Leibniz's thought is that, assuming that bodies are substances, they must have a principle of identity that underwrites their continued existence as the very same substances. This principle Leibniz takes to follow from the *inesse* principle, as he makes clear in a letter to Arnauld in a discussion of personal identity (See *Supp.* 17).

In the *Discourse* this *a priori* basis is found for substances generally in the principle that everything that is true of a substance at any time is contained in its full concept or individual essence. It is in virtue of this theory of substance, introduced in   §8, that Leibniz professes to be rehabilitating substantial forms.

19 See *Discourse* 34–5.

20 This is a reference to the principle of **inesse* (see Introduction, Section 4).

21 See §7 above.

22 At this point Leibniz added a note on his manuscript: 'The passage from Plato's *Phaedo* in which Socrates ridicules Anaxagoras, who introduces a mind but makes no use of it, should be inserted.' Following Gerhardt and Lestienne we have included it here. The passage translated here concludes a short paper by Leibniz against seventeenth-century naturalism (G viii 333–6). It is his own (slightly abridged) French translated of *Phaedo* 96b–99c. The rest of the paper is included in this edition as *Supp.* 9.

23 In his 'Theory of Abstract Motion', part of his *New Physical Hypothesis*, published in 1671 (see PPL 139 ff., G iv 228 ff).

24 In his 'A Unifying Principle of Optics, Catoptrics and Dioptrics', *Acta Eruditorium*, 1682.

25 This is discussed in §22. For a fuller (though later) account of the importance Leibniz attached to final causes in the natural sciences, see Supp. 10.

26 Willebrord Snell (1580–1626) was a Dutch mathematician, geographer, astronomer and worker on optics. He is best known for his discovery of the long sought-for sine law for the bending of light at the surfaces of transparent bodies. Descartes, who was the first to publish this law, was suspected by some — including Leibniz (see *Supp.* 10) — of having known of Snell's results and of having worked out his own account with the benefit of hindsight.

27 Heliodorus of Larissa was a minor Greek mathematician of whom little is known as who was probably known to Leibniz because of a work doubtfully attributed to him in an edition of 1657.

28 Pierre de Fermat (1601–65) was a French mathematician who invented a system of **analytical geometry independently of Descartes. He worked extensively on number theory, probability and optics. His work on the maxima and minima of algebraic functions makes him a precursor of Leibniz and Newton in their work on the differential calculus.

29 In *Supp.* 11 Leibniz credits the argument to early Scholastics and suggests that Descartes merely revived it (see *Meditations* VI). In this *Critical Thoughts on the General Part of the Principles* (1692) Leibniz expressly (*à propos Principles* Part I, Articles 14) claims that Anselm, in this book *Against the Fool*, was the first to discover and state this argument.

30 The distinctions outlined in this section are explained more fully (and slightly differently) in Leibniz's 'Meditations on Knowledge, Truth and Ideas' (1684), included here as *Supp.* 11.

31 Leibniz had Hobbes in particular in mind. Earlier he had written a dialogue criticizing Hobbes' position. See PPL 182–5, G vii 190–3.

32 It is likely that Leibniz had Descartes in mind, since Descartes defines an idea as 'the form of any thought' in a work with which Leibniz was familiar (in his geometric demonstration of God's existence given in reply to the Objections collected by Mersenne). On this account an idea is that in virtue of which one thought is to be distinguished from another.

33   The view that ideas are immediate objects of our thoughts existing outside our minds in one put forward by Malebranche in his *Search after Truth*, Book III, Part 2, and was one of the issues taken up by Arnauld. Leibniz was sympathetic to Malebranche's position (see *Supps.* 11 and 12) but agreed with Arnauld that ideas are 'modifications of our soul'.

34   Leibniz here alludes to the Scholastic Aristotelian maxim: *'nihil est in intellectu quod non fuerit in sensu'*. In the *New Essays* (p. 111) he added his own rider, *'nisi ipse intellectus'* remarking that 'an exception must be made of the soul and its states' and therefore of various notions included in the soul such as being, substance, one, same, cause, perception and reasoning.

35   Leibniz here quotes from the Vulgate: *'lumen illuminans omnem hominem venientem in hunc mundum'* (*John* 1:9).

36   Here Leibniz uses a Latin phrase: *'intellectus agens animae rationalis'*.

37   Guillaume de St Amour (*c.* 1200–73), Canon of Bejauron, taught philosophy at the University of Paris and belonged to the Sorbonne at its foundation.

38   Leibniz has Malebranche in mind at this point, as is clear from the corresponding part of the paper (*Supp.* 11) he contributed to the debate between Arnauld and Malebranche over ideas. See also *Supp.* 12 for a later tribute to and criticism of Malebranche.

39   Leibniz uses a Latin phrase *'altitudinem divitiarum'* whose source in the Vulgate (*Romans* 11:33) would have been familiar to many of his readers. This passage from St Paul is alluded to again at the end of §31.

40   Here Leibniz quotes a Latin source: *'quos se fide donatorum praescivit'*.

41   §§14–15 above.

42   Leibniz has St Theresa in mind. He once went so far as to have a correspondent believe that one of his hypotheses (perhaps the one put forward in this paragraph) was an application of St Theresa's thought to philosophy. (*Grua*, 1948, p. 103). The connection, if there was one, was probably much more complicated.

43   See §14 above.

44   What follows is a string of New Testament quotations and allusions, with some of Leibniz's main metaphysical conclusions mixed in: 'Are not sparrows two a penny? Yet without your Father's leave not one of them can fall to the ground. As for you, even the hairs of your head have all been counted. So have no fear; you are worth more than any number of sparrows' (Matthew 10:29–30); 'Heaven and earth will pass away; my words will never pass away' (Mark 13:31); 'Do not fear those who kill the body, but cannot kill the soul. Fear him rather who is able to destroy both soul and body in hell' (Matthew 10:28); 'I tell you this: there is not a thoughtless word that comes from men's lips but they will have to account for it on the day of judgement' (Matthew 12:36); 'And if anyone gives so much as a cup of cold water to one of these little ones, because he

is a disciple of mine, I tell you this: that man will assuredly not go unrewarded' (Matthew 10:42); '... and in everything, as we know, he co-operates for good with those who love God and are called according to his purpose' (Romans 8:28); 'And then the righteous will shine as brightly as the sun in the kingdom of their Father' (Matthew 13:43); 'But, in the words of Scripture, "Things beyond our seeing, things beyond our hearing, things beyond our imagining, all prepared by God for those who love him"' (I Corinthians 2:9).

Supplementary texts

These short texts and extracts have been chosen for the light they throw on the *Discourse*. They are largely arranged in sections that correspond to the main phases of the *Discourse* itself. We have chosen texts where Leibniz explains himself more fully than he does in treating some topics in the *Discourse*. Where possible we have chosen texts of the period. But in several cases, where we judged there was no great change in outlook or doctrine, we have selected extracts from Leibniz's later writings. It will be apparent, for instance, that Leibniz was later to put an even greater stress on his 'principle of the perfection of God's operations' and on the usefulness of final causes in natural science than he did in the *Discourse*.

We have not chosen later texts to show points of contrast with the *Discourse*. But we have concluded with a selection of other expositions and explanations Leibniz wrote of his system in the 1686–7 period. These are included partly for comparison and contrast, as is a journal paper of 1684 that overlaps in content with the *Discourse* treatment of ideas.

A¹ Intimations of the 'Short Discourse on Metaphysics' (early 1686)

1 *Leibniz's announcement of the work*
(Extract from a letter to Count Ernst von Hesse-Rheinfels, February 1686, G ii 11)

This is the letter in which Leibniz first mentioned that he had written the *Discourse* and in which he asks for a summary of it to be sent to Arnauld. Hesse-Rheinfels was a Catholic and, like Leibniz, was keen to see a reconciliation between the Catholic Church and the Lutherans (Leibniz's denomination). Had Arnauld been able to approve the theological content of the *Discourse* Leibniz would have been able to use it further in his project of reconciliation. (Leibniz mentions that Arnauld would be a kind of 'censor'). In this respect the project was a failure, though Arnauld was willing to continue the correspondence on philosophical matters and indeed made many good critical points about Leibniz's system as presented to him. Leibniz attached a particular value to this correspondence and at one time considered publishing it, together with the *Discourse*.

We include four extracts (*Supp.* 7, 8, 15 and 20) from letters sent by Leibniz to Arnauld.

I have just written a short discourse on metaphysics — for several days I was somewhere with nothing to do — and I would be happy to have Arnauld's opinion on it. For questions of grace, the *concurrence of God with creatures, the nature of miracles, the cause of sin and the origin of evil, the immortality of the soul, ideas etc. are handled in a way that seems to give new openings towards clarifying very great difficulties.

I attach a list of [the] contents of its articles, for I have not yet been able to get a fair copy made. So I beg your Serene Highness to have it sent to him with the request that he consider it a little and give his opinion on it. For, as he excels equally in theology and in philosophy, in reading and in meditation, I can find nobody more appropriate than him to judge it. I strongly desire a censort as exact, as enlightened, and as reasonable as Arnauld, since I am the most willing man in the world to give way to reason. Perhaps Arnauld will find these few things not altogether unworthy of his consideration, particularly since he has been much occupied with examining these matters. If he finds some obscurity, I will explain myself frankly and openly, and finally, if he finds me worthy of his instruction, I will act in a way that will leave him no reason for dissatisfaction. I beg your Serene Highness to attach this [letter] to the list of contents I am sending him, and to send both to Arnauld.

2   Summary of Discourse (G ii 12–14)

This text is the summary as sent for the attention of Arnauld. It differs slightly from the headings added by Leibniz to the text of the *Discourse*.

1. Of divine perfection; God does everything in the most desirable way.

2. Against those who maintain that there is no goodness in the works of God or that the rules of goodness and beauty are arbitrary.

3. Against those who think that God could have done better.

4. Loving God calls for complete satisfaction with and acquiescence in what He does.

5. What the rules of the perfection of the divine conduct consist in; simplicity of ways is balanced by richness of effects.

6. God does nothing outside of the *order and that it is not possible even to imagine events that are not regular.

7. Miracles conform to the general order although they are contrary to *subaltern* norms; what God wills or permits, and of general and particular wills.

8. In order to distinguish the actions of God from creatures, I explain what the notion of an individual substance consists in.

9. Each unique substance expresses the whole universe in its own way, and its notion includes all events that happen to it, with all their circumstances and the whole *sequence of external things.

10. There is something sound about the theory of *substantial forms, though these make no difference to the appearances and should not be employed to explain particular effects.

11. The meditations of the theologians and philosophers known as *scholastics are not to be despised altogether.

12. The notions defined by extension involve something imaginary and could not constitute the substance of body.

13. Since the individual notion of each person includes once for all everything that will ever happen to him, in it are found the *a priori* proofs or reasons for the truth of each event, or why one happened rather than the other; but though these truths are assured they do not cease to be contingent, since they are based on the free will of God and of creatures. It is true that there are always reasons why they are chosen, but they *incline without necessitating.

14. God produces various substances according to the different views he has of the universe; each substance's own nature ensures by God's intervention, that what happens to one corresponds to what happens to all the others, without them acting directly on each other.

15. The action of one finite substance on another consists solely in the increase in the degree of its *expression combined with the diminution of that of the other, in that God formed them in advance so that they would conform to each other.

16. The extraordinary *concurrence of God is included in what our *essence expresses, for that expression extends to everything, but it exceeds the powers of our nature or distinct expression, since that is finite and follows particular *subaltern norms.

17. Example of a *subaltern norm or † law of nature, where it is shown that God always regularly conserves the same force, but not the same quantity of motion; against the Cartesians and some others.

18. Importance of the distinction between force and quantity of motion, *inter alia*, in deciding that we must have recourse to metaphysical considerations apart from extension in order to explain the *phenomena of bodies.

19. Usefulness of *final causes in physics.

20. Memorable passage of Socrates in Plato's *Phaedo* against excessively materialist philosophers.

21. If mechanical rules depended on geometry alone without metaphysics, the *phenomena would be quite different.

22. Reconciliation of the two ways, of which one goes by final causes, and the other by *efficient causes, to answer both those who explain nature *mechanically and those who have recourse to incorporeal natures.

23. Returning to immaterial substances; the explanation of how God acts on the understanding of minds and of whether we always have the idea of what we think.

24. What is clear or obscure, distinct or confused, adequate or inadequate, intuitive or suppositive knowledge, and what are nominal, real, causal and essential definitions.

25. In what case our knowledge is joined to the contemplation of the idea.

† reading 'ou' for 'du'

26.   We have all ideas in us; Plato's notion of reminiscence.

27.   How our souls can be compard to empty tablets and how our notions come from the senses.

28.   God alone is the immediate object of our perceptions existing outside us and He alone is our light.

29.   Nevertheless we do think directly through our own ideas and not by those of God.

30.   How God *inclines our souls without necessitating them; we have no right to complain; we must not ask why Judas sins (since that free action is included in his notion) but only why the sinner Judas is admitted to existence in preference to some other possible persons; the imperfection or original limitation before sin, the degrees of grace.

31.   The motives of election, faith foreseen, the *middle knowledge, everything reduces to the reason why God chose and resolved to admit one possible person to existence whose notion includes one particular sequence of graces and free actions. This brings all the difficulties to an end at once.

32.   Usefulness of these principles in matters of piety and religion.

33.   Explanation of the interaction between soul and body, formerly accepted as inexplicable or miraculous; the origin of confused perceptions.

34.   On the difference between minds and other substances, souls and substantial forms; the immortality called for implies memory.

35.   The excellence of minds: God considers them in preference to other creatures; minds express God rather than the world and other simple substances *express the world rather than God.

36.   God is the monarch of that most perfect republic composed of all minds and the happiness of this city of God is His principal object.

37.   Jesus Christ has revealed to men the mystery and admirable laws of the Kingdom of Heaven and the greatness of the supreme happiness God prepares for those who love Him.

B The principle of 'the perfection of the operations of God' (*Discourse* §§1–7)

3 On Descartes's conception of God (Extract from an undated letter, c. 1679, G iv 299ff., translated from Robinet, pp. 116ff.)

> This extract is a part of a general assessment of Descartes. Its tenor is similar to that of 'Two sects of naturalists' (*Supp.* 9). Another extract from the same letter is included as *Supp.* 16. It brings out the link between the early sections of the *Discourse* and those later sections (§§17–22) where Leibniz is concerned to defend purposive ('final cause') explanations in natural science. It also brings out the extent to which the *Discourse* is directed against Descartes and the Cartesians even at points where they are not actually mentioned.

It will be said to me that Descartes establishes the existence of God so well ... I fear that we are being fooled by fine words. For the God, or perfect Being, of Descartes is not the God we imagine, and hope for, Who is just and wise and does everything possible for the good of His Creatures, but rather something like the God of Spinoza, namely the principle of things and a kind of sovereign power called primitive Nature that sets everything going and does everything that can be done, but has neither *will* nor *understanding*, since for Descartes he has neither the *good* for the object of His will, nor the *true* for the object of His understanding. Thus, he will not have his God act according to some end, and that is why he removes the search for *final causes from philosophy, on the crafty pretext that we are incapable of knowing the purposes of God. Plato, in contrast, who showed so well that God is the author of all things and that if God acts according to wisdom, the true physics is the knowledge of the purposes and uses of things, for science is the knowledge of reasons and the reasons for what is made by understanding are the final causes or plans of He who made them; and these appear from their use and the function they fulfil. That is why in anatomy the consideration of the use of the parts is final.

That is why a God made like that of Descartes leaves us no other consolation than that of forced patience. In several places[1] he says that matter passes successively through every possible form, that is, his God does everything that can be done and passes in accordance with a necessary and pre-determined order through every possible combination. But for that material necessity alone would be enough, or rather his God is nothing other than that necessity, or this principle of necessity acting in matter as it can. Hence it must not be believed that this God has more care for intelligent creatures than for others. Everyone will be happy or unhappy according as he is wrapped up in the great vortices: he is right to recommend to us (instead of happiness) patience without hope.

4   *The Perfection of God and His creation*
    (From *Principes de la Nature et de la Grace, fondés en raison*,
    1714, G vi 602–3)

> This extract from a much later work shows Leibniz's continuing preoccupation with some of the main themes of the *Discourse*, especially the perfection of the world (see *Discourse* §5) and the importance of final causes in science (see *Discourse* §19).

7.   Whereas up to now we have been speaking only as physicists, we must now rise to metaphysics. To do so we make use of the *grand principle*, ordinarily little used, which requires that *nothing happens without a sufficient reason*, i.e. without it being possible for someone with an adequate knowledge of things to give a reason sufficient to determine why they are that way and not otherwise. Given this principle, the first question that can legitimately be asked will be; '*Why is there something rather than nothing?*', since nothing is simpler and easier than nothing. Moreover, supposing that things have to exist, we must also be able to give a reason, *why they must exist in that form*, and not otherwise.

8.   Now this sufficient reason for the existence of the universe could not be in the system of contingent things, i.e. of bodies and their representations in souls, because as matter is in itself indifferent to motion and rest, and to one motion as against another, *the* reason for Motion, and even less that for a particular motion, is not to be found in it. And although the present motion of matter comes from the previous motion, which in turn comes from the motion previous to it, that does not get us further forward, however far we go in that direction: the same question remains. So the sufficient Reason, which has no further need of another reason, must be outside the *system of contingent things and in a substance that is the cause of that system, or else in a

necessary Being having the reason for Its existence within It. Otherwise we would not yet have a sufficient reason at which we could stop. This ultimate Reason for things is called God.

9.   This simple primitive substance must contain to the highest degree the perfections contained in the derivative substances which are its effects. Thus it will have perfect power, knowledge and will, i.e. omnipotence, omniscience and supreme goodness. And since in a very general sense *justice* is nothing more than goodness conforming to wisdom, there must indeed also be supreme justice in God. The Reason that brought things to exist through Him also makes them depend on Him in their existence and operation, and from him they continually receive what gives them some kind of perfection, though what remains imperfect in them derives from the essential original limitation of creatures.

10.   It follows from God's supreme perfection that when He produced the universe He chose the best possible plan, in which there is the greatest variety and the greatest order: with land, site, and time best arranged, the maximum effect produced by the simplest ways; the most power, the most knowledge, the most happiness and goodness in creatures that the universe could admit of. For all possibles claim existence in God's understanding in proportion to their perfections, so that the result of all these claims must be the most perfect possible real world. Without that it would be impossible to give a reason why things have gone this way rather than otherwise.

11.   God's supreme wisdom led Him to choose above all those *laws of motion* that were best adjusted and most appropriate to abstract and metaphysical reasons. In it He conserves the same quantity of total absolute force or action, the same quantity of relative force or reaction, and the same quantity, lastly, of directive force. Moreover, action is always equal to re-action and the total effect is always equivalent to the complete cause. It is surprising that by considering *efficient causes* or matter alone it is impossible to account for the laws of motion discovered in our time and in whose discovery I had a share.[2] For I found that we had to have recourse to *final causes*, and that these laws did not depend on the *principle of necessity*, like the truths of logic, arithmetic and geometry, but on the *principle of appropriateness*, i.e. wise choice.

This is one of the most effective and persuasive proofs of the existence of God for those able to go deeply into these things.

5 Miracles, laws of nature and the will of God
(From *Essais de Theodiceé*, 1710, G vi 238–41)

> This extract brings out the importance of Malebranche's philosophy and its problems for the topics discussed in the *Discourse*. Here is a fuller explanation of the distinction between general and particular wills (see *Discourse* §7) and of the connection between this topic, Leibniz's account of miracles and laws of nature and his criticism of Malebranche's account of the mind-body relation (§33).

204.   After moving from philosophy to theology, the exellent author of the *Recherche de la Vérité* finally published a very fine treatise on nature and grace. In it, he showed in his way (...) that events deriving from the implemention of the general laws are not the object of a particular will of God. Though it is true that when we will a thing in a way we also will everything necessarily connected to it, so that God could not will the general laws without in a way also willing all the particular effects that must necessarily derive from them, it is also true nevertheless, that we do not will these particular events for their own sake. That is what is meant by saying that we do not will them by a *special* direct *act of will*. There is no doubt that when God decided to act beyond His self, He close a method of acting worthy of His supremely perfect Being, i.e. infinitely simple and uniform while yet being of infinite fertility. It can even be imagined that this way of acting by *general acts of will* seemed to Him preferable to a more detailed alternative way of acting, in his view {Malebranche's}, even though it had to result in some superfluous events (or even, I would add, ones that are evil when taken on their own).

....

206.   I agree with the Revd. Father Malebranche that God makes things in the way most worthy of Him, but I go further than him in the matter of *general and particular wills*. As God could do nothing without reasons, even when acting miraculously, it follows that He has no will concerning individual events that is not a consequence of a truth or general will. So, I would say that God never has *particular wills* within his {Malebranche's} meaning, I mean absolutely particular will.

207.   I even believe that there is nothing to distinguish miracles as such from other events, because reasons which are superior to the order of nature lead God to perform them. So, I should not follow him [Malebranche] in saying that God departs from the general laws whenever order requires: He only departs from a law in accordance with another more applicable law, and what order requires cannot fail to conform to the rule of order, which is one of the general laws. What is characteristic of miracles (in the most rigorous sense of the word) is that they cannot be explained by the natures of created things. That is why, if God made a law that bodies should attract each other, he could only obtain its execution by perpetual miracles. In the same way, if God wanted the organs of human bodies to conform to the wills of the soul, according to *the system of *occasional causes* that law too could only be carried out by means of perpetual miracles.

208.   So we must conclude that from among the general rules that are not absolutely necessary, God chooses the ones that are most natural, those most easy to account for, and those most useful also in accounting for other things. That, beyond doubt, is what is most beautiful and attractive, and even if *the system of pre-established harmony*³ were not otherwise necessary, in the absence of superfluous miracles, God would have chosen it because it is the most harmonious. The ways of God are the simplest and most uniform: it is because He chooses the rules that limit each other least. They are also the most *fertile* in relation to *the simplicity of the ways*. It is as if we said that a house was the best that could be built for the same cost. We can even reduce these two conditions, simplicity and fertility, to one single advantage, the production of as much perfection as possible: by this means the Revd. Father Malebranche's system in this respect reduces to mine. For if the effect were supposed greater, but the ways less simple, I think that it could be said that when everything was weighed and accounted for, the effect itself would be not so great, when we consider, not just the final effect, but also the intermediate effect. For He who is most wise acts so that as far as possible the means should in some way be fine as well, i.e. desirable, not only because of what they produce, but also because of what they are. The more elaborate ways use too much ground, too much space, too much place and too much time which could be put to better employment.

C   The system of created substances
(*Discourse* §§8–11)

6   *On the distinction between God and His creatures*
(From *De ipse natura* §10, *Acta Eruditorum*, September, 1698, G iv 509f.)

> This extract brings out the post-Cartesian context of the *Discourse*, throwing particular light on the difficulty of distinguishing God from the creatures (§8). It also brings out the context of Leibniz's theory of the interrelation of substances (§14) and his theory of the mind-body relation (§33).

But not let us consider rather more carefully the view of those who deny to created things a true activity of their own — the view once held by Robert Fludd, the author of the *Mosaic Philosophy*, and now by some of the Cartesians. They think that it is not [sc. created] things that truly act, but God. God acts in the presence of things and in accordance with the fitness of things, so that things are *occasions and not causes and merely receive actions as opposed to producing or eliciting them. After Cordemoy, La Forge and other *Cartesians had put forward this doctrine, it was Malebranche especially, with his gifted intelligence, who elaborated a clear defence of it. But no one, to my knowledge, has put forward sound reasons for this doctrine. Certainly, if it is pushed as far as denying immanent[4] actions in substances ... then nothing appears so foreign to reason. For who will doubt that the mind thinks and wills, that many thoughts and volitions are elicited in us and by us, and that there is a spontaneity about us? To do this would be to deny human freedom and to throw the blame for evil onto God. It would also contradict the evidence of our inner experience and consciousness, on the strength on which we take to be our own what these dissenters transfer to God without any reason. But if we ascribe to our own minds the indwelling power to produce immanent actions — or, what is the same thing, of acting immanently, then there is no objection at all to the same force residing in other souls or forms or, if you prefer, in the nature of substances. And yet someone might judge that only minds are active in the world we know or that all power of acting immanently (and hence 'vitally', so to speak) is conjoined with an intellect. Such assertions are not supported by any reason and can be defended only by imposing on the truth. As to what can be maintained about the *transeunt[4] actions of creatures*, that can be better expounded elsewhere. In fact we have already explained it in part — *the communication of substances* or monads does not arise from an *influx but from an agreement that has its source in how they were preformed by God. Each one is accommodated to the others while, at the same time, it follows the indwelling power and laws of its own nature. It is in this too that *the union of soul and body* consists.

7 The unity of substance
(From a letter of Arnauld, April 1687, G ii 96, translated from *Lewis*, pp. 69–70)

That substances are indivisble unities seems initially to be a
consequence (see *Discourse* §9) of Leibniz's account of what a substance
is rather than a prior requirement. The correspondence with Arnauld
brought out, however, that for Leibniz it is a requirement of something
being a substance that it be a true unity, what is referred to in *Discourse*
§34 as an *unum per se*. In this extract Leibniz defends his making it a
definitional requirement of something being counted as a 'substance'
that it be a true unity.

If my opinion that substance requires a true unity were founded merely on a definition I had forged counter to common usage, 'it would be merely a dispute about words', unless I had not thereby noticed or distinguished thereby a notion underservedly neglected by others, but besides the fact that the common philosophers have taken this term in almost the same way 'in distinguishing a unity by itself from an accidental unity, and a substantial form from an accidental, imperfect mixtures from perfect, natural from artificial'. I have taken things from a much higher level and terminology aside: I believe that 'wherever there are only beings by aggregation, there will not even be real beings'. For, every aggregate being supposes beings endowed with true unity, because it takes its reality only from that of those it is composed of, so that there cannot be any at all if every being it is composed of is still an aggregate being, or else some other basis must be sought for its reality. If we must continue to seek it in this way this reality can never be found. I agree, Sir, that in all corporeal Nature, there is nothing but machines (often animated), but I do not agree that 'there are only aggregates of substances', and if there are aggregates of substances, there must necessarily also be true substances from which all these aggregates are made. Hence we must necessarily return, either to the mathematical points from which some writers make up extension, or to the atoms of Epicurus or Cordemoy (things you agree with me in rejecting), or else we must admit that there is no reality in bodies; or finally we must accept substances that possess a true unity. In another letter I have already said that the composite of the diamonds of the Grand Duke and the Great Mogul can be called a pair of diamonds, but that is a being of reason only, and when they are brought together it will be a being of imagination or perception, that is a *phenomenon. For contact, common motion, and coming together in the same design make no difference to substantial unity. It is true that according as the things are more connected, there is sometimes more basis and sometimes less for supposing several things to make one single thing, but that is useful for abbreviating our thoughts and representing the *phenomena only.

8   *The nature of 'expression'*
    (From a letter to Arnauld dated 9 October 1687, G ii 111–3, translated from *Lewis*, pp. 78–80)

    The theory of expression is an integral part of Leibniz's account of substance in the *Discourse* (§§14–16). In this extract he offers a further explanation of what he means by 'expression'.

I had said that since in a certain sense the soul naturally expresses the whole universe according to the relation of the other bodies to its own, and since consequently it expresses more directly what belongs to the parts of its body, it must, in virtue of the laws of relation essential to it, particularly express extraordinary motions of the parts of its body — which happens when it feels pain. Your reply to this is that you do not have a clear idea of what I intend by the word *express*. If by it I understand a thought, you do not agree that the soul has more thought and knowledge of the motion of the lymph in the lymphatic vessels than of the satellites of Saturn, but if I understand something else, you do not, you say, know what that is, and hence (supposing that I cannot distinctly express it) this term will be of no help in explaining how the soul can obtain the sensation of pain, since for that (as you claim) it would have to know already that I was being pricked, whereas it only has that knowledge through the pain it feels. In reply, I will explain the term you judge obscure, and apply it to the difficulty you have raised. In my terms, one thing expresses another when there is constant and regular relationship between what can be said of each one. Thus it is that a perspective projection expresses its plane[†] projection. Expression is common to all forms, and is a genus of which natural perception, animal sense, and intellectual knowledge are the species. In natural perception and in sense it is enough that what is divisible and material, and is divided into several beings should be expressed or represented in a single indivisible being, or in a substance endowed with true unity. [The possibility of a beautiful representation of several things in a single one cannot be doubted since our soul gives us an example of it, but] that representation is accompanied by consciousness in the rational soul, and that is when it is called thought. Now this expression occurs everywhere, since all substances sympathise with all others and are changed in proportion to the least change occurring anywhere in the universe, though this change may be more or less appreciable to the extent that the other bodies or their actions have a greater or smaller relation to ours. This is something I believe Descartes himself would have agreed with, for he would certainly have accepted that in consequence of the continuity and divisibility of all matter the least movement extends its effect to neighbouring bodies and hence, though proportionately diminished, from neighbour to neighbour *ad infinitum*. Hence our body must in some way be affected by the changes in all others. Now to all movements of our body there correspond particular perceptions or thoughts, more or less confused, in our soul. So the soul too will have some thought of every movement in the universe ...

D   The importance of final causes (*Discourse* §17–22)

9   *Two sects of naturalists* (from an undated paper of the late 1670s, G vii 333ff.)

Leibniz wrote his *Discourse on Metaphysics* partly as a corrective to two kinds of 'naturalistic' philosophy that were prevalent in the seventeenth century. This text identifies these as a form of

[†] translating 'geometral' which refers to plan, elevation and profile in technical drawing.

Epicureanism (represented by Hobbes), on the one hand, and a form
of Stoicism (represented by Descartes), on the other. As in the
Discourse (e.g. §20) Leibniz finds Plato's *Phaedo* a valuable corrective
to these 'over-materialist philosophers'.

There are two sects of naturalists in fashion today deriving from
antiquity: the one has revived the opinions of Epicurus, while the
other is in truth *Stoic. The first believe that all substance,
including the soul and even God, is corporeal, i.e. material or
extended mass. From this it follows that there cannot be an all-
powerful and all-knowing God, for how could a body act on
everything without being affected by everything and without being
corrupted? This has been well recognised by one Vorstius,[5] who
denied his God all those great attributes other men ordinarily give
theirs. Some have believed that the sun was God, since judging by
the senses it is beyond contradiction the most powerful of visible
things, but they did not know that all the fixed stars are as many
suns, so that as a result one alone could neither see nor do
everything. Every body is heavy and very powerful if it is big, and
very weak if it is small, or if (like gunpowder) it is very powerful
despite its smallness, it destroys itself when it acts. That is why a
body cannot be God. So Epicurus in times past and Hobbes today,
who claim that all things are corporeal, have sufficiently testified
that for them there is no Providence.

In the belief of the new Stoic sect there are incorporeal
substances: human souls are not bodies; God is the soul, or, if you
will, the first power of the world, and, if you like, the cause of
matter itself, but He is determined to act by blind necessity. That
is why He will be in the world what the spring or the weight is in
the clock. For them there is a mechanical necessity in things, and it
is by power indeed, rather than by the reasonable choice of this
Divinity, that things act, since properly speaking God has neither
understanding nor will, which are the attributes of men. For them
all possible things happen one after the other in accordance with
all the varieties matter is capable of, final causes must not be
looked for, and there is no certainty as to either the immortality of
the soul or the future life. For them there is no justice with God,
and it is His decision that determines goodness and justice. Hence,
as a result, He would be doing nothing contrary to justice if He
always made the innocents wretched. That is why these gentlemen accept Providence in name only, and as far as concerns

results and the conduct of our lives, everything comes back to the opinion of Epicurus, i.e. there is no other happiness than the tranquility of a contented life here below just as it is, since it is folly to resist the torrent of things and not be content with what cannot be changed. If they knew that all things are ordered for the general good and the particular happiness of those who can make use of it, they would not place happiness in mere patience. I know that their expressions are very different from some of those I have just set out, but when their opinions have once been penetrated to their foundations, what I have just said will be granted. These indeed are the opinions of Spinoza, and Descartes seems to many people to be of the same opinion. Certainly he rendered himself very suspect by rejecting the search for *final causes, by maintaining that there is neither justice, goodness, nor even truth except because God so determined it absolutely, and finally by letting slip (although in passing) that all the possible varieties of matter happen successively one after the other.[6]

While these two sects of Epicureans and Stoics are dangerous to piety, that of Socrates and Plato, which derives (in my belief) partly from Pythagoras, is the more conformable to it. We have only to read the admirable dialogue of Plato on the immortality of the soul to notice in it opinions altogether opposed to those of our new Stoics. In it Socrates speaks on the very day of his death, shortly before receiving the fatal cup. By marvellous reasoning he banishes the sadness from the minds of his friends by replacing it with admiration, and he seems merely to be leaving this life to enjoy in another the happiness prepared for fine souls. I think, he says, that by going I will find better men than those here, but I am sure at least of going to find the gods. He maintains that final causes are the most important in physics and that it is these that must be searched for in accounting for things. And he seems to bait our new physicists when he baits Anaxagoras. What he says deserves to be heard ...

[The quotation from Plato's *Phaedo* that follows has been inserted in *Discourse* §20 above — eds.]

10   *The importance of Final Causes in natural science* (From *Essay Anagogique dans la recherche des causes* — also entitled *Tentamen Anagogicum*, though it was written in French, around 1696, G vii 270–4)

This unpublished essay develops some themes of *Discourse* §§19–22. Although the utility of final causes in the sciences had been stressed by Leibniz, at least as early as his 1682 paper on 'A Single Principle for Optics, Catoptrics and Dioptrics' (alluded to in *Discourse* §21), it came to be stressed increasingly by him as he saw further applications of the thought that 'the true physics should in fact be derived from the source of the divine perfections' (PPL353 G iii 54). What we include as the first paragraph was added by Leibniz at a later stage and provides a synopsis of what follows.

What leads to the Supreme Cause is called 'anagogical' in the writings of both philosophers and theologians. So here it is first shown that there is no accounting for the laws of nature without the supposition of an intelligent cause. That is, it is shown also that in the search for final causes there are causes where we must have regard for the simplest and most determinate without distinguishing whether it is the largest or smallest. The same thing is also found in the differential calculus, and the general law of direction of the ray drawn from *final causes gives a good example, irrespective of whether it is a case of reflection or refraction and whether the surface is curved or plane. From it some new general theorems are drawn applicable equally to refraction and reflection. It is shown that the analysis of the law of nature and the search for causes leads us to God i.e. it is shown how both in the way of final causes and in the differential calculus we do not consider only the largest and the smallest but generally the most determinate or simple.

I have indicated on several occasions that the ultimate resolution of the laws of nature leads us to more sublime principles of order and perfection which indicate that the universe is the effect of a universal intelligent power. This knowledge is the chief fruit of our researches, as the ancients recognised; without mentioning Pythagoras and Plato, who made it his chief concern, even Aristotle tended, by his works, particularly his *Metaphysics*, to demonstrate a Prime Mover. It is true that, not being as instructed as us in the laws of nature, the ancients lacked many of the means we have and must profit from.

The knowledge of nature gives birth to art; it gives us many means of preserving our life; it even gives us comforts for it. But in addition to being the greatest pleasure of this life, the satisfaction of the mind which derives from wisdom and virtue also raises us to things eternal when this life is so short. Consequently, what serves for establishing rules that find happiness in virtue and derives everything from the principle of perfection, is infinitely more useful to man and even to the state than what serves the arts. So discoveries useful in life are very often only corollaries of more important insights, and it is true here too that those who search for the kingdom of God find the rest on the way.

To search for final causes in physics is to practise just what I believe we ought to do, and those who tried to banish them from their philosophy did not give enough thought to their great usefulness. For I do not want to do them the wrong of thinking that they meant harm thereby. However, there have been others who exaggerated. They have not been content with excluding final causes from physics and instead of referring them elsewhere they have tried to destroy them altogether and to show that the Author of things, though in truth all-powerful, was without intelligence. There are yet others who accepted no universal cause, like those ancients who saw in the universe only the collisions of corpuscles. This is something plausible to minds in which the imaginative faculty predominates, because they think they have only to employ the principles of mathematics without needing to employ the principles of metaphysics, which they call chimerical, nor those of goodness, which they refer to human morality, as if perfection and goodness were only a particular effect of our thoughts, and not in universal nature.

I recognise that it is easy to fall into this mistake, especially when in meditating we limit ourselves to what the imagination alone can supply, i.e. sizes and shapes and their modifications; but when the search for reasons is continued it is found that the laws of motion could not be explained by principles of pure geometry or of the imagination alone. It is this also that has made some very able philosophers of our time believe that the laws of motion are purely arbitrary. They are right in this if they take to be *arbitrary* what derives from choice and is not subject to geometrical necessity, but we should not extend this notion so far as to believe that these laws are altogether indifferent, since it can be shown that they have their origin in the wisdom of the Author, or in the principle of the greatest perfection, which caused them to be chosen.

This consideration supplies us with the just mean needed to satisfy both truth and piety. We know that if there have been able

philosophers who saw in the universe only what is material, there
are on the other hand learned and zealous theologians, who in
their shock at the corpuscular philosophy, and not content to
remedy its abuses, have felt themselves obliged to maintain that
there are phenomena in nature, such as light, weight and elastic
force, that cannot be explained by the principles of mechanics. But
as they do not reason here with exactness, and it is easy for the
corpucular philosophers to answer them, they damage religion
when they think they are serving it, since they confirm those who
accept only material principles in their error. The just mean that
must satisfy both of them is that while all nature phenomena can
be explained mechanically if sufficiently understood, the actual
principles of mechanics cannot be explained geometrically, since
they depend on more sublime principles pointing to the wisdom of
the Author in both the order and the perfection of the work ...

Moreover, our meditations sometimes provide us with
considerations showing the use of final causes not only for
increasing the admiration of the Supreme Author, but also for
making discoveries in His work. I once[7] showed this by way of
example when I proposed a general principle of optics that the ray
passes from one point to another by the easiest path with respect
to plane surfaces (to which to other surfaces have to be referred).
For it must be realised that if we claimed to employ this principle
as an *efficient cause, and as if all possible rays competed against
each other and the easiest won out, we would then have to
consider the surface as it is irrespective of the plane touching it
[N.B. mechanical analogy of equilibrium of forces]. In that case, as
will shortly be said, the attempt will not always succeed. But far
from hiding the fact that this principle has something about it of
the final cause, the objection once made to Fermat who used it in
his *dioptrics, I find it finer and of more weight for more sublime
use than mechanism. An able author publishing a work on optics
in England[8] has expressed his approval of me for it. Order requires
that curved lines and surfaces be treated as made up of straight
lines and planes, and a ray is determined by that plane on which it
falls that is considered as forming the curved surface at that point.
But order also requires that the effect that is easiest should be
obtained at least in those planes that serve as elements of other
surfaces, when it cannot be obtained with respect to the latter too,
particularly because with respect to them it then satisfies a second

principle that follows from the first and states that failing the minimum we must use the most determinate. Even when it is the maximum this can be the simplest.

Now it happens that the ancients and Ptolemy, amongst others, had already made use of this hypothesis of the easiest path for the ray incident on a plane to account for the equality of the angles of incidence and reflection, the foundation of *catoptrics. It was by the same hypothesis that Fermat accounted for the sine law of refraction or (stating it another way with Snell) the secant law. For it is known that Willibrord Snell, one of the greatest geometers of his time and well versed in the methods of the ancients, was its inventor and had even written a work that was not published because of its author's death. But as he had taught it to his disciples, in all probability Descartes learned of it when he arrived in Holland shortly afterwards, more curious as he was in these matters than anyone. For since the way he tried to account for it by efficient causes or by the composition of directions (of motion) in imitation of the bouncing of balls is extremely forced and not quite intelligible, to say no more here, it is obvious that it is a reasoning worked out after that fact, adjusted somehow to the conclusion, and that it was not found by this means. So that it is to be believed that we would not have had this fine discovery so soon without the method of final causes.

E The Nature of Ideas (*Discourse* §§23–29)

11 Meditation on knowledge, truth and ideas
   (Paper entitled '*Meditationes de cognitione, veritate et ideis*', originally published in *Acta Eruditorum*, November 1684, G iv 422–6)

> Leibniz's philosophical thinking in the period prior to writing the *Discourse* was much affected by the controversy between Malebranche and Arnauld over true and false ideas. This is Leibniz's only published intervention in the controversy. He had already begun to study the exchanges in part and was to make extensive notes on them in 1685. The controversy between Malebranche and Arnauld reflects the different ways in which they built on the work of Descartes. In this paper Leibniz states, and claims to be able to remedy, what he regards as the defects in Descartes's account of 'clear and distinct ideas'.

The question of true and false ideas is of great importance for understanding the truth and is one to which Descartes himself never gave a satisfactory answer. Since it currently provokes controversy amongst distinguished men, I would like to explain in a few words my own account of the different kinds of ideas and knowledge and their criteria. Knowledge, then, is either obscure or clear, and in turn clear knowledge is either confused or distinct and distinct knowledge is either inadequate or adequate as well also as symbolic or intuitive. Whatever knowledge is at the same time adequate and intuitive is the most perfect.

A notion is obscure when it is not enough for recognising the thing represented as when I recall having seen some flower or animal but not well enough to recognise a specimen or distinguish it from a related one. Another example is where I give thought to some term that the Scholastics defined poorly such as Aristotle's Entelechy, or cause, understood as what is common to material, formal, efficient and final causes or other terms such as these of which we have no certain definition. When a proposition contains such a concept it too becomes obscure. Accordingly knowledge is clear when I am able by means of it to identify the thing represented and clear knowledge, in turn, is either confused or distinct. It is confused when I cannot enumerate separately the marks that are sufficient to distinguish the thing from others, even though the thing may have such marks and requisites into which its notion can be resolved. Thus we identify colours, smells, flavours and other particular objects of the senses clearly enough and distinguish them from one another but only by the simple testimony of sense and not by marks that can be articulated. Thus we cannot explain to a blind man what red is, nor can we explain such a quality to others except by confronting them with the object and making them see, smell or taste it, or at least by reminding them of a similar perception they have had before. Nonetheless it is certain that the concepts of these qualities are composite and can be analysed in so far as they have, of course, their own causes. In a similar way we sometimes see painters and other artists who rightly judge that something is done correctly or is faulty and yet who are unable to give a reason for their judgment except to tell the questioner that the work they dislike lacks 'something, I don't know what'.

A distinct notion, on the other hand, is the kind of notion which assayers have of gold, which, that is to say, enables them to distinguish gold sufficiently from all other bodies by sufficient marks and features. We are familiar with such concepts in the case of objects common to many senses such as number, magnitude and figure and also in the case of many mental dispositions such as hope and fear — in the case, in short, of all concepts of which we have a *nominal definition*, which is nothing but an enumeration of sufficient marks. We may also have a distinct knowledge of an indefinable concept, however, when this is *primitive* or is the sign of itself — when, that is to say, it is irreducible and to be understood only through itself and therefore lacks *requisites. In composite concepts however, the individual component marks are indeed sometimes known clearly but nevertheless confusedly, such as heaviness or colour, *aqua fortis*, and other marks of gold. Such knowledge of gold may therefore be distinct and yet it is *inadequate*. When every ingredient that enters into a distinct concept is itself known distinctly or when the analysis is carried out to the end, knowledge is *adequate*. I am not sure that a perfect example of this can be given by man, but we come near to it with our notion of numbers. And yet in the main, especially in a longer analysis, we do not have in mind the entire nature of a thing at once, but make use of signs instead of things. Usually, for the sake of brevity, knowing or believing that we have the power to explain these signs, we omit the explanations of them. Thus when I think of a chiliagon, or a polygon of a thousand equal sides, I do not always consider the nature of a side, of equality and of a thousand (or the cube of ten) but I use these words (whose meaning is obscurely and imperfectly before the mind) in place of the ideas I have of them. I remember that I know the meaning of the words but their explanation is not needed for the present judgment. Such thinking I usually called *blind* or *symbolic*. We use it in algebra and in arithmetic and indeed just about everywhere. And certainly it is not possible for us to think simultaneously of all the constituent notions that make up a very complex notion. And yet, where this is possible — for at least to the extent that it is possible, I call this *intuitive* knowledge. In the case of distinct primitive notions there is no other knowledge than intuitive. In the case of composite notions there is, for the most part, only symbolic thinking.

From this it is already manifest that we do not perceive the ideas even of those things we know distinctly except in so far as we use intuitive thought. And it is bound to happen that we are often mistaken in believing ourselves to have ideas in our mind when we wrongly suppose we have already explained certain terms we are using. It is not true or it is at least ambiguous to say, as some do, that we cannot speak about something, understanding what we say, without having an idea of it. For we often understand each individual word to some extent or recall having understood it previously: yet, because we are content with this blind thinking and do not push far enough the analysis of notions, it can turn out that a contradiction involved in a complex motion escapes our attention. I was led into considering this matter more distinctly by an argument for the existence of God which was much used by the scholastics long ago and was revived by Descartes.[9] It runs as follows:

Whatever follows from the idea or definition of a thing can be predicated of the thing itself. Existence follows from the idea of God (or the most perfect being, or that than which no greater can be thought). (For a most perfect being includes all the perfections amongst them also existence.) Therefore existence can be predicated of God.

On a true account, this much follows from this argument: if God is possible, it follows that He exists. For we cannot safely draw conclusions from definitions until we know that they are real or that they involve no contradiction. The reason for this is that from notions that involve a contradiction, it is possible to draw opposite conclusions, which is absurd. I usually illustrate this point with the example of the most rapid motion, which involves an absurdity. For suppose that a wheel turns at its most rapid movement. Who cannot see that if a spoke of the wheel is extended beyond its rim, its extremity will move more quickly than will a nail in the circumference of the wheel. The motion of the nail is therefore not the fastest, contrary to our hypothesis. Yet at first sight we may seem to have an idea of a fastest motion, for we understand just what we are saying. Yet we cannot have an idea of something impossible. Likewise it is not enough to think of a most perfect being in order to claim that we have an idea of it, and in the above demonstration we must either prove or assume the possibility of a most perfect being in order to argue soundly. However nothing is more true than that we have an idea of God and that the most perfect being is possible, even necessary. But the above argument is not conclusive and it was already rejected by Aquinas.[10]

In this way we can distinguish between *nominal definitions*, which contain only marks for distinguishing one thing from others, and real definitions from which the possibility of the thing is settled. In this way we can meet the objection of Hobbes who held truths to be arbitrary because they depended on nominal definitions, failing to consider that the reality of a definition does not depend on our arbitrary choice, and that not all concepts can be combined with one another. Nominal definitions are not enough for perfect knowledge unless it has been established in some other way that the defined thing is possible. It becomes obvious what is a true idea and what is a false one. It is true when the notion is possible and false when it involves a contradiction. Now we know the *possibility* of a thing either *a priori* or a *a posteriori*. We know it *a priori* when we analyse a notion into its requisites or into other concepts whose possibility is known, and we know that there is no incompatibility between them. This happens, amongst other ways, when we understand how something can be produced and so *causal definitions* are more useful than others. We know an idea is true *a posteriori* when we experience a thing as an actual existence — for what actually exists or has existed is assuredly possible. And when we have adequate knowledge we also have *a priori* knowledge of what is possible, for if we have carried out the analysis to the end, and no contradiction has become manifest, the notion is assuredly possible. Whether man will ever be able to carry out a perfect analysis of notions to reduce them to the *first possibles* or irreducible notions, or (what comes to the same thing) the absolute attributes of God themselves, or the first causes and ultimate rasons for things, I shall not presume to determine.[11] For the most part we are content, having learnt the reality of certain concepts from experience, to compose other concepts out of them following the example of nature. From this therefore I believe it can be understood that it is not always safe to appeal to ideas and that many thinkers have abused this deceptive word in order to set up the products of their imaginations. The example of the fastest motion has already shown that we do not always at once have an idea of something of which we are consciously thinking. Nor is it any less of an abuse, I think, when a man of our time advanced the principle: whatever I perceive clearly and distinctly about something is true or can be stated of that thing. For what seems clear and distinct to men when they judge rashly is frequently obscure and confused. Thus the axiom is useless unless the criteria of clearness and distinctness that we have brought forward and adduced and unless the truth of the ideas is established. As for the rest, the rules of *common logic* — which even geometricians use — should not be despised as criteria of the truth of statments. So, for example, nothing is to be admitted as certain unless it is proved by accurate experiment or by sound demonstration. A demonstration is sound when it follows the form prescribed by logic though it need not always follow the form of syllogisms arranged in the scholastic manner (such as Christian Herlinas and Conrad Dasypodius[12] applied to the first six books of Euclid). All that is necessary is that the argument be valid by virtue of its form. Any proper calculation could be mentioned as an example of argumentation carried forward in the proper form. Accordingly no necessary premise is to be left out and all premises must either be proved in advance or at least admitted to be hypotheses, in which event the conclusion is also hypothetical. Whoever observes these rules diligently will be able to guard himself easily against deceptive ideas. The ingenious Pascal quite agrees with this in his outstanding dissertation on the Geometrical Spirit (a fragment of which is extant in the outstanding book of that celebrated man Antoine Arnauld on the *Art of Thinking*) that a geometrician ought to define all his terms even if they are only slightly obscure and to prove all his propositions even if they are only slightly doubtful. I only wish he had defined the limits beyond which a notion or judgment as no longer even slightly obscure or doubtful. This can nevertheless be gathered by careful attention to what we have said. For we are now taking care to be brief.

As for the controversy whether we see all things in God — an old opinion and one that, properly understood, is not wholly to be spurned — or whether each of us has our own ideas, it should be understood that even if we saw things in God it would still be necessary for us to have ideas ourselves — not like little copies but affections or modifications of our mind corresponding to the very thing we perceive in God. For whenever thoughts follow on one another there are also ideas of things in our mind of which we are not actually thinking rather as the figure of Hercules is in the rough marble. But in God there must be not only the ideas of absolute and infinite extension but also of every shape since shape is nothing but a modification of absolute extension. Furthermore when we perceive colours or smells we are having nothing but a perception of shapes and motions but ones that are so complex and tiny that our mind in this present state is not able to observe each distinctly and so fails to notice that its perception is made up of individual perceptions of tiny figures and motions. So, when we mix yellow and blue powders and perceive a green colour, what we sense is nothing but yellow and blue minutely mixed, only we do not notice this and so assume mistakenly that there is something new.

12 On Malebranche's system

(From a letter to Nicolas Remond dated 4 November 1715, G iii 659–60, translated from *Robinet*, p. 481)

Although Malebranche had been a highly influential and even fashionable thinker in the last decades of the seventeenth century, he became increasingly the target for adverse criticism. In this letter Leibniz is largely concerned to defend Malebranche against Rodolfe Du Terte's *Refutation*. Although Leibniz disagreed with Malebranche on a number of important points it is clear from this extract that there was much in common between them — too much, perhaps, for Leibniz to allow a sweeping dismissal of Malebranche's philosophy to pass without comment.

(8) It is more plausible to oppose the opinion of Father Malebranche on ideas. For there is no necessity (it seems) to take them for something outside us. It is enough to consider ideas as notions, i.e. modificaitons of our soul. That is how they are taken in the schools, by Descartes and by Arnauld. But since God is the source of possibilities and hence of ideas, we can excuse and even praise him for having changed the terms and given ideas a more exalted significance by distinguishing them from notions and taking them for perfections in God in which we participate by our knowledge. [11] His mystical language, then, was not necessary but I find it useful, for it makes us better envisage our dependence on God. It even seems that when Plato talked of ideas and Augustine of truth they had almost the same thoughts, and I find them very reasonable. It is the part of Father Malebranche's system that I would be happy to see preserved along with the expressions and formulations that depend on it, just as I am also happy that the most solid part of the theology of the mystics should be preserved. Far from saying, with the author of the *Refutation* (Vol 2, 304),

that 'the system of St Augustine is somewhat infected with Platonic language and opinions', I would have said that it is enriched and set off thereby.

(9)   I would say almost the same of Father Malebranche's opinion when he claims that we see everything in God. I say that it is an expression that can be excused and even praised, provided that it is taken in the right way, for it is easier to go wrong here than in the preceding article on ideas. Hence it is good to remember that, not only in Father Malebranche's system, but also in mine, God alone is the immediate external object of souls, exerting a real *influence on them. Although the ordinary *scholastics seem to accept other influences, by species of some kind, which they believe to be sent by the objects into the soul, they do not cease to recognise that all our perfections are a continual gift of God and a finite participation in His infinite perfection. This suffices to conclude that even what is true and good in our knowledge is an *emanation of the light of God, and that in this sense we can say that we see things in God.

F   Application of these principles to religion
(*Discourse* §§30–32)

13   Divine foreknowledge and human free will
      (From *Essais de Theodiceé sur la Bonté de Dieu, la Liberté de l'Homme et l'Origine du Mal*, Part I, §§38–47, 1710, G vi 4–9)

In *Discourse* §§13, 30 and 31, Leibniz alludes to a cluster or problems arising from the assumption that God is wholly perfect, and therefore both all-knowing, and all-powerful, and proposes solution to them. The *Theodicy* enters into some of the details of the theologically-dominated debates of Scholastic philosophy to which Leibniz merely alludes in the *Discourse*.

But see what an opponent could say: I grant you that foreknowledge does not in itself make the truth more determinate, but it is the cause of the foreknowledge that makes it so. For it is very necessary that God's foreknowledge should have its basis in the nature of things, and since this basis makes the truth predetermined, it will prevent it from being contingent and free.

39. It is this difficulty that gave birth to two parties: the *predeterminationists* and the defenders of the *middle knowledge*. The Dominicans and the Augustinians are for predetermination, while the Franciscans and the modern Jesuits are more for the middle knowledge. These two parties arose about the middle of the sixteenth century and shortly afterwards. Molina himself (perhaps, with Fonseca, one of the first to put this point into a system and from whom the others were called Molinists) says in his book on the harmony of freewill and grace (about 1570), that the Spanish Doctors (he means chiefly the *Thomists) who had written in the previous twenty years had introduced predeterminations as necessary to free actions because they found no other way of explaining how God could have a certain knowledge of future contingents.

40. As for him, he thought he had found another way. He considers there are three objects of divine *knowledge*; possibles, real events, and conditional events that will occur in consequence of a particular condition if that were brought to actuality. The knowledge of possibilities is what is called *the knowledge of simple intelligence*; that of events really occurring in the sequence of the universe is called the *knowledge of vision*. Since there is a kind of mean between the simple possible and the pure and absolute event, that is the conditional event, we may also say, according to Molina, that there is a *middle knowledge* between that of vision and that of intelligence. Of this the famous example is given of David, who asked the divine oracle if the inhabitants of the town of Kegila, where he planned to take refuge, would hand him over to Saul if Saul laid siege to the town. God's answer was yes, and on that David took a different course. Now some defenders of this middle knowledge consider that since God foresees what men would freely do, if they were placed in such and such circumstances and knows that they would make wrong use of their free will, He makes a decree to refuse them favourable circumstances and grace. He can rightly so decree, since both these circumstances and assistances would have been no use to them. But Molina contents himself with finding in this a reason in general for the decrees of God based on what the free creature would do in such and such circumstances.

41. I do not go into the detail of this controversy: it is enough to give a sample of it. Some ancients, with whom St Augustine and his first disciples were not happy, seem to have had thoughts close enough to those of Molina. The *Thomists and those called by themselves disciples of St Augustine (but *Jansenists by their adversaries) attack this doctrine philosophically and theologically. Some claim that the middle knowledge ought to be included in the knowledge of simple intelligence. But the main objection goes against the basis of this knowledge. For, what basis can God have for seeing what the Kegilites would do? There is nothing about a free contingent act able in itself to yield a principle of certitude unless it is considered to be predetermined by the decrees of God and causes depending on these. Hence the difficulty with real free actions recurs with conditional free actions, i.e. God will only know them on the basis of their causes, and of His decrees which are the primary causes of things. Moreover these cannot be detached from it in order to know a contingent event, in a manner independent of the knowledge of causes. Hence all must be reduced to the predetermination of the decrees of God, so that this middle knowledge, it will be said, will be of no help. The theologians who profess attachment to St Augustine also claim that the Molinist procedure would make the source of God's grace lie in the good qualities of men, something they judge contrary to the honour of God and the doctrine of St Paul.

42. It would be lengthy and boring to go here into the replies and retorts made on one side and the other, and it will be enough to explain how I conceive that there is truth on both sides. To that end I return to my principle that there is an infinity of possible worlds, present in the region of eternal truths, i.e. in the object of the divine intelligence where all future contingents must be included. For the case of the siege of Kegila is part of a possible world *differing from ours only in respect of everything connected with this hypothesis*, and the idea of this possible world represents what would happen in this case. Hence we have a principle of the certain knowledge of future contingents whether they really happen or whether they have only to happen in a particular case. For, in the region of possibles they are represented such as they are, i.e. free contingents. Hence it is not the foreknowledge of future contingents, nor the basis of the

certainty of that foreknowledge that should cause us embarassment or prejudice freedom. Even if it were true that the future contingents consisting in the free actions of reasonable creatures were entirely independent of the decrees of God and external causes, there would still be means for foreseeing them, for God would see them just as they are in the region of the possibles before decreeing to admit them to existence.

43.   But if the foreknowledge of God has nothing in common with the dependence or independence of our free actions, it is not the same with God's preordination and his decrees, and with the sequence of causes which I believe always contributes to the determination of the will. And if I am for the Molinists on the first point, I am for the predeterminators on the second, while, though, constantly observing that predetermination does not necessitate. In a word, I am of the opinion that the will is always more inclined to the side it takes but never under the necessity of taking it. It is certain that it will take this side, but not necessary that it will take it. This is in imitation of the famous saying 'the stars incline but do not necessitate' although the case is not altogether the same. For the event to which the stars carry (I speak with the vulgar as if there were some basis for astrology) does not always happen, whereas the side to which the will is most inclined does not fail to be taken. So the stars form no more than a part of the inclinations concurring in the event, but when we speak of the greatest inclination of the will we are speaking of the result of all the inclinations, nearly the same as we spoke above of the consequent will of God which results from all previous acts of will.

44.   Nevertheless objective certainty or determination does not entail the necessity of the truth determined. All philosophers recognise this when they admit both that the truth of future contingents is determined and yet that they do not cease to be contingent. The thing would imply no contradiction in itself if the effect did not follow, and it is in this that *contingency* consists. To understand this point better, we must remember that there are two great principles in our reasonings: the one is the *principle of contradiction*, which entails that of two contradictory propositions one is true and the other false; while the other *principle* is that of *the determining reason*, which is that nothing ever happens without a cause or at least a determining reason, i.e. something

that can serve for giving an *a priori* reason why it is existent rather than non-existent, and thus rather than otherwise. This great principle applies in every event and a contrary example will never be given. Although most often these determining reasons are not sufficiently known to us, we do not fail to glimpse that there are such. Without this great principle we could never prove God's existence, and we would lose an infinity of very sound and useful reasonings based on it. It is free from exception or otherwise its force would be weakened. Moreover, there is nothing so feeble as these systems in which everything is rickety and full of exceptions. That is not the fault of the one I support in which everything goes by general rules which at most limit each other.

45.   Hence we must not imagine with some *scholastics, who tend a little to the chimerical, that free future contingents are privileged with respect to this general rule of the nature of things. There is always a prevailing reason to carry the will to its choice, and to preserve its liberty, it is enough that this reason *inclines without necessitating. This was also the opinion of all the ancients, of Plato, of Aristotle and of St Augustine. The will is never brought to act except by the representation of the good, which prevails over contrary representations. It is agreed even with regard to God, good angels and blessed souls, while it is still accepted that they are not the less free. God does not fail to choose the best, but he is not forced to do so, and there is not even any necessity in the object of God's choice, for another sequence of things is equally possible. It is for this very reason that the choice is free and independent of necessity, that it is made between several possibles and the will is determined only by the superior goodness of the object. So it is not a fault in relation to God and the saints — on the contrary it would be a great fault, or rather a mainfest absurdity if it were not so, even in men here below, if they were capable of acting without any inclining reason. That is why no example will ever be found and when a side is taken capriciously to show our freedom, the pleasure or advantage found in that affectation is one of the reasons leading to it.

46.   Hence there is a liberty of contingency, or in a way, indifference, provided that by *indifference* it is understood that nothing necessitates us towards the one side or the other; but there never is a *balanced indifference*, i.e. one in which everything is equal on

each side, without any greater inclination towards one side. An infinity of great and little internal and external motions concur with us, which we are most often unaware of. I have already said that when we leave a room there are reasons that determine us without reflection to put a particular foot first. For nowhere is there a slave, as in Trimalcion's house in Petronius, to shout to us 'Right foot first'. Everything we have just said also agrees perfectly with the maxims of the philosophers, who teach that a cause could not act without a disposition to act, and it is this disposition that contains a predetermination, whether the agent has received it from outside, or he has possessed it in virtue of his own previous constitution.

47. So, there is no need, with some modern *Thomists, to have recourse to a new direct predetermination of God making the free creature leave his indifference, and to a decree of God to predetermine it, to give God the means of knowing what it will do; for it is enough that the creature should be predetermined by his previous state, which inclines him more to one side than to the other. All these connections of actions of the creature and all creatures were represented in the understanding of God and known to God by simple intelligence, before He gave the decree to give them existence. This shows that to account for the foreknowledge of God we can do without both the *middle knowledge of the Molinists, and predetermination, such as a Bannus or an Alvarez[13] (authors who are otherwise very profound) have taught.

14 *Accommodating theology as well as physics*
    (the concluding comments from Leibniz's *Animadversiones in partem generalem Principiorum Cartesianorum*, 1692, G iv 390–2)

Leibniz did not make a careful study of Descartes's *Principles of Philosophy* until after he had written the *Discourse*. But he wrote many critical appraisals in the 1690s in which, as in the *Discourse*, he sought to recommend his own philosophy in contrast with that of Descartes.

The author ends the second part of his book, which is a general treatment of the principles of material things, with a remark that seems to me to call for qualification. He insists that that no other principles are necessary for the explanation of natural phenomena than those taken from abstract mathematics, or from size, shape and motion, and that the only matter that should be recognised is what is the subject of geometry. I fully agree that all the particular phenomena of nature can be explained mechanically if they are sufficiently explored by us and that it is not possible to understand the causes of material things on any other basis. Nonetheless I hold that we should consider how these mechanical principles themselves as well as the general laws of nature arise from still higher principles and cannot be explained in quantitative or geometrical terms. Rather there is something metaphysical about them which is independent of the notions afforded by the imagination and which is to be referred to an extensionless substance. For as well as extension and its variations there is in matter the force or power of action which makes the transition from metaphysics to nature, from material to immaterial things. This force has its own laws that are derived from principles not only of absolute and so the speak brute necessity, as in mathematics, but from those of perfect reason.

Once these matters have been settled in a general way we may then go on to explain everything *mechanically in accounting for the phenomena of nature and it is as vain here to introduce the perceptions and appetites of an *arché, operative ideas, *substantial forms, and even souls, as it is to invoke the universal cause of all things, a *deus ex machina*, who will move individual natural things by a simple act of willing, as I recall the author of *The Mosaic Philosophy*[14] does by means of a misinterpretation of the words of Holy Scripture.

Anyone who considers the matter honestly will hold to the middle road in philosophy and give satisfaction to theologians no less than to physicists. He will appreciate that the *scholastics went wrong of old not so much in adhering to indivisible *forms as in applying them when they ought rather to have been looking for the modifications and means of substance, its mode of action, that is, mechanism. It is as if nature has an empire within an empire, a double kingdom, so to speak of reason and of necessity, or of *forms and of particles of matter, for just as all things are full of souls so they are full of organic bodies. These kingdoms are governed each by its own law, with no confusion between them. No more is the cause of perception and appetite to be sought in the modes of extension than is the cause of nutrition and of other organic functions to be sought in forms or souls. But that highest substance, which is the universal cause of all things, brings it about in conformity with His infinite wisdom and power, that two very different series in the same substance correspond to one another and are in perfect harmony with one another, just as if one were ruled by the influence of the other. And if attention is given to the necessity of the matter and the order of *efficient causes nothing will be found without a cause that satisfies the imagination and nothing that lies outside the mathematical laws of mechanism. If, on the other hand, the golden chain of ends and the circle of forms is contemplated as an intelligible world, they are united in one on account of the perfection of their supreme Author. Ethics and metaphysics meet together at the apex since nothing happens without the highest reason, the same God being both the supreme form and the first efficient cause the end or ultimate reason of things. Our concern is to pay homage to His traces in nature and to meditate not only on His means in operating and the mechanical efficacy of material things, but also on the more sublime uses of His admirable craftsmanship. It is our concern to acknowledge God as in a manner the architect of bodies, but most importantly as king of minds whose understanding orders everything for the best and makes the universe the most perfect republic under the dominion of the most powerful and most wise monarch. Thus we take care of both considerations to do with the particular phenomena of nature, both welfare in life and the perfection of our minds, taking care no less of wisdom than of piety.

G The nature and 'excellence' of spirits (*Discourse* §§33–37)

15 *The hypotheses of 'concomitance' and 'occasional causes'*
(From a letter to Arnauld dated 30 April 1687, G ii 92–6, translated from *Lewis* 64–8)

> In this extract Leibniz presses his criticism of 'the hypothesis of *occasional causes' and defends his own account of the relation between mind and body. In the *Discourse* account Leibniz speaks of 'correspondence' (§§14 and 23) whereas he here speaks of 'concomitance'. It was not till later that he settled on the more well-known phrase 'pre-established harmony'.

You say, Sir, that those who maintain the hypothesis of *occasional causes, when they say 'that my will is the occasional cause of the movement of my arm and God the real cause, do not claim that God does this in time by a new act of will, one that he performs every time I want to raise my arm, but by a single act of the eternal will by which he wanted to do all he foresaw he would need to do.' My reply to this is that by the same argument we could say that even miracles do not happen by a new will of God, since they conform to his general plan, and in my previous letters I have already remarked that every will of God includes all the others, though in a particular order of priority.

In fact, if I understand aright the opinion of the supporters of *occasional causes, they do introduce a miracle, and one not less so for being continual. For I feel that the notion of miracle does not consist in rarity of occurrence. It will be said to me that God only acts in this in accordance with a general rule, and consequently in a non-miraculous way, but I do not accept this conclusion, and I believe that God is able to make himself rules even relating to miracles. Thus for example if God resolved to give His grace directly, or to perform another action of that kind at every occurrence of a particular case, this action would not cease to be miraculous, although it was subject to order. I admit that the supporters of *occasional causes could define the term differently, but I feel that in ordinary usage miracles differ internally and substantially from common actions, and not by the external accident of frequent repetition, and that properly speaking God only performs a miracle when He does something beyond the powers He gave to creatures and preserves in them. [For example if God were to make it that a body once launched into circular motion by means of a sling, continued freely to travel in a circular line when released from the sling without being pulled or pushed by anything at all, this would be a miracle, since in accordance with the laws of nature, it ought to continue in a straight line along the tangent; and if God were to decree that always to happen, he would be making natural miracles, since such a motion could not be explained by something more simple.] Hence [in the same way] if the continuation of the motion exceeds the body's force, it must be said, according to the accepted notion, that the continuation of the motion is a true miracle, whereas I believe that corporeal substance has the force to continue its changes in accordance with the laws God put in nature and preserves there. To make myself clearer, I believe that the actions of minds make no difference at all in the nature of bodies, nor bodies in that of minds, and even that God makes no changes on their occasion unless he effects a miracle. In my opinion, things are so co-ordinated that no mind ever wants anything efficaciously, unless the body is ready to do it in virtue of its own laws and powers[: whereas according to the supporters of *occasional causes, God changes the laws of bodies on the occasion of the soul and *vice versa*. This is essential difference between our opinions.] Thus[, according to me,] there is no need to worry about how the soul can give a motion or some new determination to the animal spirits, since in fact it does not ever do so, as much because there is no proportion between mind and body as because there is nothing able to decide what degree of speed a mind will give a body, or even what degree of speed God should want to give to a body on the occasion of a mind following some law, since the same difficulty arises in relation to the hypothesis of occasional causes, as in that of a real *influence of the soul on the body *and vice versa*, since no connection or basis for any rule can be seen. It might be said, and this seems to have been Descartes's understanding, that the soul, or God on the occasion of it, changes only the direction or determination of the motion, and not the force in the body, since it did not seem probable to him that at every moment on the occasion of each of the wills of minds God violated the general law of nature that the same force must subsist. My reply is that it would still be difficult enough to explain what connection there could be between the thoughts of the soul and the sides or angles of the directions of bodies. Moreover there is yet another general law in nature that Descartes was not aware of, and is no less important: that the same determination or direction in total must always subsist in nature. For I find that if any straight line whatever is drawn, e.g. from east to west through a given point, and if the directions of every body in the world are calculated, to the extent that they advance or recede along straight lines parallel to this line, the difference between the sums of the quantities of all the easterly directions and that of the westerly directions would always be the same, whether between some particular bodies, supposing that they alone are now in mutual interaction, or in relation to the whole universe. Here the difference is always zero, since everything is in balance and the easterly and westerly directions are perfectly equal in the universe. If God does anything against this rule, it is a miracle.

Hence it is infinitely more reasonable and more worthy of God to suppose that in the beginning he created the machine of the world in such a way that without at any moment violating the two great laws of nature, namely those of force and direction, but rather following them perfectly (except in the case of miracles), it happens that just at the moment that the springs of the bodies are ready to move of themselves as they should, the soul has an appropriate thought or will that it too had solely in conformity with the preceding states of the bodies. The union of the soul with the machine of the body and the parts entering into it, and the action of the one on the other thus consists only in this concomitance, which is a much better mark of the admirable wisdom of the Creator than any other hypothesis. It cannot be denied that this is at least possible, nor that God is a skilful enough workman to be able to carry it out. Hence it is easy to decide that this hypothesis is the most probable. It is the most simple, the most beautiful and the most intelligible. At one stroke, it removes all the difficulties, to say nothing of criminal actions, where it seems more reasonable not to make God give *concurrence except by the conservation of created forces alone.

Lastly, to use a comparison, I will say of this concomitance maintained by me, that it is like several different bands of musicians or choirs separately playing their parts and so placed that they neither see nor even hear each other, but are nevertheless able to harmonise perfectly by following their notes, each its own, so that he who hears them all finds in them a marvellous harmony that is much more surprising than if there were a connection between them. It could even happen that someone, at the side of one of the two choirs, could tell by the one what the other was doing, and got so habituated to this (particularly if it is supposed that he could hear his one without seeing it, and see the other without hearing it), that because his imagination filled the gap, he ceased to think of the choir he was with, but of the other, or took his own for no more than the echo of the other and attributed to the one he was with only some intervals in which the rules of harmony by means of which he judged the other were absent; or else he attributed to his own particular movements he had arranged in accordance with his plans and believed to be imitated by the others because of the relationship he found in the sequence of the melody, in ignorance of the fact that those on the other side were doing still other appropriate things as they followed their own plans.

Nevertheless I in no way disapprove of minds being called in some way occasional or even real causes of bodily motions; for in respect of divine resolutions, what God foresaw and pre-ordained for minds, was an occasion making him regulate in this way the bodies at the beginning so that they would conspire with each other in accordance with the laws and powers he gave them. And since the state of the one is an unavoidable consequence [of the other], although often contingent and even free, it can be said that God makes it that there is a real connection, in virtue of that general notion of substances which implies that they all perfectly express each other. But this connection is not direct[, since it is based only on what God did when he created them].

16 *Descartes's account of immortality*

(From the same undated paper as 'Descartes's conception of God' (*Supp.* 3), G iv 300f., translated from Robinet, p. 117f.)

Leibniz here elaborates on a topic treated briefly in *Discourse* §34, on the virtues of his own and the inadequacies of Descartes's account of immortality.

But perhaps one of the more honourable of the Cartesian gentlemen will say, deceived by his master's fine talk, that he does establish so well the immortality of the soul and consequently a better life. When I hear these things, I am astonished at how easy it is to fool the world merely by craftily playing on agreeable words, although their sense is corrupted. For, just as the hedonists misuse piety, the heretics Scripture, and the seditious the word liberty, so the Cartesians have misused these great phrases, the existence of God and the immortality of the soul. Hence this mystery must be unravelled and they must be shown that the immortality of the soul in Descartes's sense is worth hardly more than his God. I know well that I will give some people no pleasure. For people do not like being woken up when their minds are occupied by agreeable dreams. But what is to be done? Descartes wants us to uproot false thoughts before introducing the true. His example must be followed and I believe I will be rendering the public a service if I am able to disabuse them of such dangerous doctrines.

Hence, I claim that the immortality of the soul as established by
Descartes is useless and could in no way console us. For,
supposing the soul is a substance and no substance perishes, then
the soul will not be lost, as indeed, nothing in nature is lost. But
since just like matter the soul will change its manner of being, and
since just as the matter composing a man once composed plants
and other animals, in the same way, this soul may indeed be
immortal, but it will pass through a thousand changes and will be
not remember what it has been. Such immortality without
memory is altogether useless for morality, for it upsets all reward
and punishment. What use, Sir, would it be to you to become
King of China on condition that you forgot what you had been?
Would it not come to the same thing if God, at the same time as he
destroyed you, created a King in China? That's why, if the hope of
the human race is to be satisfied, the hope of the human race must
be given the promise that the God who governs is altogether wise
and just and that he will leave nothing without punishment or
reward. These are the great foundations of morality.

But the doctrine of a God who does not act for the good and of
a soul that is immortal without memory serves only to deceive the
simple and pervert spiritual persons.

17 *Personal identity*
   (From remarks on a letter of Arnauld, May 1686, G ii 42–3)

> This extract, like the previous one, has a bearing on *Discourse* §34. In
> particular it brings out how Leibniz saw his theory of the individual
> substance as underwriting a meaningful immortality, that is one in
> which personal identity is retained.

It also follows that it would not have been our Adam, but another,
if he was involved in different events, for nothing stops us saying
that it was another. Hence it is another. It is evident to us that this
block of marble brought in from Genoa would have been
completely the same if it had been left there, because our senses
only make us judge superficially; but fundamentally, because of
the *connection of things, the whole universe with all its parts
would have been completely different, and would have been so
from the beginning, if the least thing had gone differently from the
way it goes. That does not mean that the events are necessary, but
that they follow with certainty from the choice God made of this
possible universe whose notion contains this *sequence of things. I

hope that what I am about to say will command the assent of even Arnauld. Let a straight line ABC represent a specific time. Let there also be a specific individual substance, me for example, remaining or subsisting during the time AB, and me still subsisting during the time BC. Since, then, it is supposed that it is the same individual substance that lasts — that is that it is me subsisting during time AB who was then in Paris, and me still subsisting during time BC who is now in Germany — there must necessarily be a reason that makes us say truly that we persist, that is that I who have been in Paris am now in Germany. For if there is not, we would have as much right to say that it was someone else. It is true that my interior experience has convinced me *a posteriori* of this identity, but there must also be an *a *priori* (reason) for it. Now it is not possible to find another unless my attributes both of the preceding time and state and of the following time and state are the predicates of the same subject, 'belong to the same subject. Now what is it to say that the predicate is in the subject unless the notion of the predicate is somehow included in the notion of the subject? And since from the time I began to be it could be truly said that this or that was happening to me, it must be admitted that these predicates were laws included in the subject or in my *complete notion, which constitutes what is called me, and is the foundation of the connection of all my different states and is known by God from all eternity. After that I believe that all doubts must vanish, for in saying that the individual notion of Adam includes everything that will ever happen to him, I do not mean anything other than what all the philosophers understand when they say 'the predicate is in the subject of a true proposition'. It is true that the consequences of such an obvious doctrine are *paradoxical, but that is the fault of philosophers who do not follow up sufficiently the consequences of the most clear notions.

H Other explanations and summaries of Leibniz's system (1686–7)

18 *From a letter to Simon Foucher (1686)* (G i 381–2)

Leibniz's friend Foucher saw himself as the reviver of a form of scepticism he associated with Plato's Academy. Foucher's strategy with works such as Malebranche's *Search After Truth* was to identity their

main 'suppositions' and then imply that since they were assumed
without proof there was no reason to believe what was being claimed.
In this letter Leibniz gives qualified support for Foucher's Academic
Scepticism and defends both his own methodology and his alternative
to Malebranche's system.

The Philosophy of the Academics, which is the knowledge of the
weaknesses of our reason, is good for the foundations, and since
we are always at the foundation in matters of religion, it is
certainly suitable for the better subjection of reason to authority.
You have shown this very well in one of your discourses.[15] But in
matters of the human sciences we must try to advance and even if
the only way to do so was by establishing many things on a few
suppositions, that is still of use: at least we should know that all
that remained to reach a full demonstration was to prove these few
suppositions, and in the meantime we should have some
hypothetical truths and escape from the confusion of disputes.
This is the method of the Geometers. For example, Archimedes
supposes only these few things: that the straight line is the
shortest; and that if two lines are everywhere concave on the same
side, the line included is shorter than the including line. On that
basis he completes his demonstrations with rigour ...

Hence, if for example we supposed the principle of
contradiction and then that in every true proposition the notion of
the predicate is included in that of the subject, and several other
axioms of this nature; and if from these we could prove many
things as demonstratively as the Geometers, would you not find
this result of consequence? But we would have to begin this
method one day if we were to begin to put an end to the disputes.
It would always be a means of gaining territory.

It is certain, even, that we must suppose some truths, or else
give up all hope of making demonstrations, for proofs could not
go to infinity. We must not ask for the impossible, otherwise we
would be giving evidence that we were not serious in searching for
the truth. Hence, I will continue to suppose boldly that two
contradictories could not be true, and that what implies a
contradiction could not be, and consequently that necessary propositions (that is those of which the opposite implies a
contradiction) have not been set up by free decree. Otherwise we
are misusing words. Nothing more clear could be produced for
proving these things. You yourself suppose them in writing and

reasoning, or else at any moment you could defend quite the opposite of what you say ...

I also feel that you are right [...] to doubt that bodies can act on minds and vice versa. On this matter I have a pleasing opinion, which seems necessary to me and is very different from that of the author of the *Recherche*. I believe that every individual substance expresses the whole universe in its manner and that its next state is a consequence (though often free) of its previous state, as if there were only God and it in the world. But since all substances are a continual production of the sovereign Being, and *express the same universe or the same phenomena, they agree with each other exactly, and that makes us say that the one acts on the other, because the one *expresses more distinctly than the other the cause or reason of the changes, rather in the way we attribute, and with reason, motion to the vessel rather than to the whole of the sea. I also draw this consequence, that if bodies are substances, they could not consist of extension alone. But that does not change our explanations of particular phenomena of nature: they should always be explained mathematically and mechanically, provided that we understand that the principles of mechanics do not depend on extension alone. Hence I am neither for the common hypothesis of the real *influence of one created substance on the other, nor the hypothesis of *occasional causes, as if God produced thoughts in the soul on the occasion of motions of the body, and so changed by a totally useless kind of perpetual miracle the course the soul would otherwise have taken. But I maintain a concomitance or agreement of what happens in the different substances, since God created the soul in the first place so that everything happens to it or arises from its own being without it having to accommodate itself to the body thereafter, no more than the body has to accommodate itself to the soul. Each following its own laws, the one freely, the other without choice, agree with each other in the same *phenomena.

19 *An undated draft commonly known as 'Primary Truths'*
    (C. 1686)
    (From *Couturat*, pp. 518–23)

In a letter to Arnauld dated 14 July 1686 Leibniz claimed that he was able to make progress in metaphysics assuming only two 'primary truths' and advancing by 'geometrical demonstrations' (G ii 62). This paper may be an attempt to make good this claim, though Leibniz seems obliged at certain points to introduce further 'suppositions'. In a letter to Foucher also written in 1686 (see *Supp*. 18) Leibniz acknowledges that in addition to the two 'primary truths' in question (the principle of contradiction and the principle that the predicate term is included in that of the subject term in every true proposition) it would be necessary to posit further 'primary truths', i.e. 'suppositions' that are put forward without proof, though he does not say what they are. But it seems as if Leibniz hoped to dispense with such further suppositions when he began writing this paper.

'Primary truths' shows a style of exposition different from that adopted in the *Discourse*. It is, from a 'scientific' point of view, more rigorous. But we should not suppose therefore that it necessarily gives a truer indication of Leibniz's way of thinking than does the *Discourse*. It may be that neither mode of exposition is wholly satisfactory from this point of view. It is characteristic of Leibniz, for example, to want to argue for the same conclusion in many different ways. Leibniz interrupts his exposition in 'Primary Truths' to observe at one point (§8) that the different arguments he gives for the same conclusion in some sense 'combine together'. This feature of Leibniz's natural style of argumentation is better accommodated by the *Discourse* than it is by 'Primary Truths'. On the other hand it is easy to read the *Discourse* and fail to see the links between what Leibniz is saying at different points. In this respect the more austere structure of 'Primary truths' makes it a helpful comparative reading.

'Primary truths' was written in Latin and its length and style suggest it may have been written for the Leipzig journal, *Acta Eruditorum*. Although it is undated there are a number of reasons in addition to those already mentioned for thinking it was written in late 1686. Paragraph numbers have been added for ease of reference.

1 Primary truths are those that state something to be itself or deny the opposite of its opposite. For example A is A or A is not non-A. If it is true that A is B, it is false that A is not B or that A is non-B. Again, everything is what it is, everything is similar or equal to itself and nothing is greater +or smaller+ than itself. These and other truths of this sort (though they may have varying degrees of importance) can nonetheless be included under the single name '*identities*'.

2 All other truths are reduced to primary truths by the aid of definitions or rather by an analysis of notions that constitutes a proof *a priori (independent of experience). I will give as an example the following proposition which is accepted as an axiom by mathematicians and all others alike: 'the whole is greater than its part' or 'a part is less than the whole'. This is

very easily demonstrated by the definition of 'less' or 'greater' together with the primitive axiom — namely, of identity. For that which is 'less' is equal to a part of another (greater) thing. This definition is very easily understood and accords with the practice of the human race when people compare things with one another and discover the excess by subtracting from the greater an amount equal to the lesser. Hence we get the following argument: a part is equal to part of the whole (namely, to itself, since everything is equal to itself, by the axiom of identity). But that which is equal to part of the whole is less than the whole (by the definition of 'less'). Therefore the part is less than the whole.

3 Therefore the predicate or consequent is always 'in' the subject or antecedent and it is in this that the nature of truth in general consists. It consists, as Aristotle also observes, in the connection between the terms of a proposition. In identities this connection and inclusion of the predicate in the subject is explicit. In all other truths it is implicit and must be brought out by an analysis of notions, which constitutes *a priori* demonstration.

4 This holds true, moreover, for every affirmative truth, whether universal or singular, necessary or contingent +and as much in the case of intrinsic denominations as in *extrinsic ones+. And here lies hidden a marvellous secret in which is contained the nature of contingency or the essential distinction between necessary and contingent truths. +It also removes the difficulty about a fatal necessity affecting even free things.+ These points have not been sufficiently considered because they are too easy. But from them follow many conclusions of great importance — for instance the received axiom *there is nothing without a reason* or *there is no effect without a cause* is immediately derived from them. For if this axiom were false a truth could be given which it was not possible to prove *a priori*, i.e. which is not analysed into identities — which is contrary to the nature of a truth, which is always expressly or implicitly an identity. It also follows that when everything, in what is given, is the same in one part as in another then everything will be the same on both sides in cases to be investigated or inferred. For no reason can be given for a discrepancy except what is sought in what is given.

A corollary, or rather, an example of this is the postulate of Archimedes at the beginning of his book on equilibrium — that when the arms of a balance and the weights put on each side are equal, everything is in equilibrium. +Hence *there is even a reason for eternal things*. If it should be imagined that the world has existed from eternity and that there were only spheres in it, a reason would be called for why there were spheres rather than cubes.+

5 From this it also follows that two individual things which differ only numerically cannot occur in nature. For it must be possible to give a reason why they are different — which needs to be sought in some difference in the things themselves. And so the point recognised by Saint Thomas that separate intelligences never differ only numerically ought to be made about other things as well. Neither two perfectly similar eggs, nor two perfectly similar leaves, nor two perfectly similar blades of grass in a garden will ever be found. And, in short, perfect similarity only has a place within complete and abstract notions where things are considered not in all their aspects but only in a limited way as when we consider shapes on their own and neglect the matter that has the shape. Thus it is right in geometry to consider two triangles to be similar even although no two perfectly similar material triangles are to be found. It is also permissible to take gold and other metals, salts and many liquids as homogeneous bodies. But that can be allowed only as far as the senses are concerned and not as if it were exactly true.

6 It also follows that *there are no +purely+ *extrinsic denominations*, which have absolutely no foundation in the thing referred to. For the notion of the subject referred to must involve the notion of its predicate. And accordingly, whenever the denomination of a thing is changed, there must be some variation in the thing itself.

7 *The complete or perfect notion of an individual substance involves all its predicates — past, present and future*. For assuredly it is already true that a future predicate will hold in the future, and so is contained in the notion of the.thing. Accordingly, in the perfect individual notion of Peter or Judas (considered merely as a possibility by abstracting the mind from the divine decree to create him) everything that will

happen to them, both necessary and free, is included and is seen by God. Thus it is obvious that God chooses from an infinite number of possible individuals those whom he judges fit best with the supreme secrets and hidden ends of His wisdom. Nor is it exactly true to say that He decrees that Peter shall sin or that Judas shall be damned. He decrees only that in preference to other possible individuals Peter who will sin (certainly, indeed, but freely and not necessarily) and Judas who will suffer damnation shall come into existence. He decrees, in other words, that the notion or possible individual shall become that of an actual individual. And although the future salvation of Peter is contained also in his notion as an eternal possibility, yet that is not without the *concurrence of grace. For in that +same perfect+ notion of this possible Peter, the support of divine grace that is to be given to him is included in the possibility being conceived.

8 Every individual substance involves the whole universe in its perfect notion and everything that exists in it — past, present and future. For there is nothing on which it is impossible to impose a +true+ denomination from something else, be it no more than one of comparison and relation. On the other hand there is no purely *extrinsic denomination. The same conclusion is shown by me in many different ways that combine together.

9 It may even be said that *all +created+ individual substances are diverse *expressions of the same universe*, and of the same universal cause which is, of course, God. But these expressions vary in perfection like different representations or perspectival drawings of the same town from diverse points of view.

10 *Every individual +created+ substance acts physically on every other and is acted on by these others*. For if there is a change in one there follows some corresponding change in all the others since the [extrinsic] denomination is changed. This accords with our experience of nature. For we see that in a vessel full of liquid (the whole universe is such a vessel) a motion produced in the middle is propagated to the edges, although it becomes more and more insensible as it goes further from its point of origin.

11 It can be said that, in strict [metaphysical] rigour, *no created*

substance exercises a metaphysical action or *influx *on another.*
For, without saying anything about it not being possible to
explain how anything can pass from one thing into the substance of another, I have already shown that all the future states
of any given thing are already implied by its notion. What we
call 'causes' are, in metaphysical rigour, only concomitant
*requisites. This is highlighted by our experience of nature,
for bodies yield to other bodies by the force of their own
elasticity and not by the force of anything else. This is true
even though another body is a *requisite for the elasticity
(which arises from something intrinsic to the body itself) to
be able to act.

12 *Furthermore, having assumed a distinction between mind and
body, we can account for their union on this basis* without the
common hypothesis of an *influx, which is unintelligible, and
without the hypothesis of *occasional causes, which calls
upon a **deus ex machina.* For God has from the beginning set
up both soul and body alike with such wisdom and skill that
because of their original nature or notion everything that
happens in the one corresponds perfectly of itself with everything that happens in the other, just as if something had
passed from the one into the other. I call this the *hypothesis of
concomitance.* This is true of all substances +in the whole
universe+ but it is not as noticeable in all of them as it is in
the case of soul and body.

13 *There is no vacuum.* For the different parts of an empty
space would be perfectly similar and congruent with one
another and would be indistinguishable, differing only numerically, which is absurd +(In the same way as it is proved that
space is not a thing, it is also proved that time is not a
thing)+.

14 [*There is no corporeal substance in which there is nothing but
extension or magnitude, shape and their variations.* For otherwise there could exist two corporeal substances that are perfectly similar to one another, which is absurd. From this it
follows that there is in corporeal substances something analogous to the soul, which is usually called a '*form'.]

15 *There are no atoms.* On the contrary there is no body that is
so small that it is not actually sub-divided. While it is itself
being acted on by every other body in the entire universe, and

receives some effect from each of them (which must cause a change in the body) it has also retained all past impressions and already contains future ones. And if anyone says that the effect is contained in the motions impressed upon an atom which receives the entire effect without itself being divided, it can be answered that not only must an effect in the atom result from all the impressions of the universe but conversely it must be possible to infer the state of the whole universe from the atom — the cause from the effect. But from the mere shape and motion of an atom we cannot argue back to the impressions that have produced a particular effect on it, since the same motion can be brought about by different impressions. This is to say nothing about the fact that it is impossible to give a reason why bodies of a particular degree of smallness are not further divisible.

16 From this it follows that *in every particle of the universe there is contained a world of infinite creatures*. The *continuum, however, is not divided into points nor is it divided in every possible way. It is not divided into points because points are not parts but limits. It is not divided in every possible way because not every creature is in the same part but only a particular infinite progression of them. In the same way someone who supposes a straight line to be divided in two parts is making different divisions from someone who supposes it divided into three parts.

17 *There is no actual determinate shape in things*. For there is no shape that can satisfy the infinity of impressions. So neither a circle or an ellipse nor any other line definable by us exists except in our intellect. Nor are there lines before they are drawn or parts before they are divided off.

18 [Space, time, extension and motion are not things but founded ways of thinking.][16]

19 Extension and motion and bodies in so far as they themselves consist of these alone, are not substances but true phenomena like rainbows and parhelia. For shapes do not exist objectively and bodies, if they are considered solely in terms of extension, are not single substances but many.

20 Something lacking in extension is required for the substance of bodies. Otherwise there would be no principle of the reality of phenomena or of true unity. There would always be

a plurality of bodies, never a single body without plurality. Cordemoy proved atoms by a similar argument. But since these have been ruled out there remains only something that lacks extension, something analogous to a soul, that used to be called 'a *form' or 'species'.

21 *A corporeal substance can neither come into being nor perish except by creation or by annihilation.* For once it endures it will always endure since there is no reason why it should be different. Nor does the dissolution of the parts of a body have anything in common with the destruction of the body itself. *Hence things that have souls do not come into being or perish. They are only transformed.*

20 *A summary of Leibniz's views* (9 October 1687)
     (From a letter to Arnauld, G ii 126–7)

This extract shows some of the influence of his correspondence with Arnauld on Leibniz's thought. Like the previous extract it contains doctrines that are closer to his later 'monadology' than anything to be found in the *Discourse* — in particular the view that there is an infinite world of creatures in every particle of matter. Arnauld apparently never received these paragraphs.

Finally, to gather up my thoughts in a few words: I hold that every substance contains in its present state all its past and future states and even *expresses the whole universe from its point of view; nothing is too remote from another to have commerce with it. This will apply particularly in connection with the relation to the parts of its own body which it expresses more directly. Consequently nothing happens to it except from its own resources and in virtue of its own laws, provided we include in this the *concurrence of God. But it perceives other things because it naturally expresses them, since it was so created in the beginning that it could do so thereafter and adjust as necessary, and it is in this obligation imposed from the beginning that what is called the action of one substance on another consists. As for corporeal substances, I hold that bulk, considered only in respect of its divisibility, is a pure appearance. In metaphysical rigour every substance is a true unity: indivisible, ingenerable and incorruptible. All matter must be full of animated or at least living substances. Generations and corruptions are only transformations of the little into the large and *vice versa*. There is no parcel of matter in which there is not an infinite world of creatures, whether organised or aggregate. Above all, the works of God are infinitely greater, more beautiful, more numerous and better ordered than is commonly believed, and the machine or organisation, that is the order, is as if essential to them, right down to the least parts. Thus there is no hypothesis that gives a better account of the wisdom of God than ours, according to which there are everywhere substances pointing to His perfection, being as many though different *mirrors of the beauty of the universe, while nothing remains empty, void, sterile, uncultivated or without perception. It must even be held as indubitable that the laws of motion and the revolutions of bodies serve the laws of justice and public order that are certainly observed as well as possible in the government of minds, that is intelligent souls, who enter into fellowship with Him and compose with Him a kind of perfect City, whose Monarch He is.

I think, Sir, that I have now neglected none of all the difficulties you had explained or at least pointed out, or even those I thought you might still have. It is true that this has lengthened my letter, but it would have been more difficult to convey the same meaning in fewer words, and obscurity might perhaps have resulted. Now I believe that you will find my thoughts sufficiently well connected, both with themselves and with those that are accepted. I do not upset established opinions, but I explain them and push them further forward. If one day you could have the leisure to review what we have finally established on the notion of an individual substance, perhaps you would find that if you granted me my principles, you would be obliged thereafter to grant me all the rest. Nevertheless I have tried to write this letter in such a way that it explains and defends itself on its own. Questions could be separated still further, for those unwilling to accept souls in animals and *substantial forms elsewhere could nevertheless approve the way I explain the union of mind and body, and everything I say of true substance. But without such forms and without anything that is a true unity, they will still have to save as they may, whether by points or by atoms, the reality of matter and corporeal substances if they want to — or even leave it unresolved. For researches can be stopped just where we want to. But we must

not stop short on such a royal road if we desire to have true ideas
of the universe and of the perfection of the works of God, that
give the soundest arguments concerning God and our souls as
well.

Notes on supplementary texts

1 One text Leibniz had in mind was *Principles of Philosophy*, Part III, Article 42, which he cites in this connection in a paper on freedom (Foucher de Careil, 1857, p. 179).

2 This is a reference to the correction to Descartes's laws of motion Leibniz first published in 1686 and which is stated in *Discourse* §17. There are slight changes in what Leibniz takes to be the implications of the discovery of this law in this passage, though it echoes the stress on the utility of final causes in physics of *Discourse* §§18–22.

3 This is the label Leibniz himself adopted for his system in his first published statement of it, his 'New system of the nature and communication of substances' (*Journal des Savants*, 1695), and which he stuck to thereafter. In the *Discourse* period he toyed with other labels such as 'the hypothesis of concomitance' (see *Supp.* 19).

4 Leibniz makes use here of a characteristically Scholastic distinction, between *immanent* actions that take place solely within a substance and *transeunt* actions that affect other substances. Leibniz himself denied only *transeunt* actions and dismissed the theory of *influx designed to explain them as unintelligible.

5 The reference is to an early seventeenth-century Dutch theologian, Conrad von der Vorst. In his *Tractatus theologicus de Deo* (1610), von der Vorst had argued that God was a definite substance and was therefore corporeal. He was banished from Holland for his unacceptable views.

6 See note 1 above.

7 In his paper '*Unicum opticae, catoptricae et dioptricae principium*', published in *Acta Eruditorum*, 1682.

8 William Molyneux, author of *Dioptrica Nova*: *A Treatise of Dioptrics*, 1709. Molyneux was in fact Irish though his book was published in London.

9 See Note 29 of Notes on *Discourse* above.

10 For instance in his *Summa contra Gentiles*, I, 10.

11 The identification of ideas (or at least simple ideas) with the perfections of God was a natural one for philosophers in the Christian Platonist tradition to make. Leibniz himself appears to endorse it in his

1684 paper (*Supp.* 11) though it is not made in the *Discourse* and he seems to have distanced himself from it in his later writings (e.g. *Supp.* 12). This identification is assumed in a version of the ontological argument Leibniz offered to Spinoza in 1676 and which he claimed Spinoza found convincing (PPL 167–8, G vii 261–2). This argument purported to prove that there was no inconsistency in the concept of God and so to meet Leibniz's own objection to Descartes's ontological argument. The fact that he ceased to use this argument later on may be due partly to his later reluctance to put any weight on the identification of ideas with God's perfections.

12   Herlinas and his pupil Dasypodius published their presentation of Euclid in syllogistic form in 1565. Dasypodius was the designer of the famous mechanical clock at Strasbourg.

13   Thomas Bañez (1528–1604) and Diego Alvarez (d. 1631) were Spanish *Thomist theologians noted for their contributions to the controversies about grace.

14   Robert Fludd (1574–1637) was a vitalist and defender of occult arts like *geomancy. His *Philosophia mosaica* was published in 1638.

15   Foucher's *Apology for the Academics* (Part I, Article 4). This work was not published until 1687 but Foucher had sent Leibniz an advance copy.

16   This is a development from the *Discourse* where material substances are assumed to be in space and space therefore in some sense a thing. Leibniz's later theory of space was stated in his correspondence with Clarke.

Glossary

active intellect
The distinction between the passive and active intellect was commonly made by the Scholastic Aristotelians. Leibniz thought, however, that it had been construed in a wrong way by *Averroes who 'believed that there is an *intellectus agens*, or active understanding, in us and also an *intellectus patiens*, or a passive understanding, and that the former, coming from without, is eternal and universal for all, while the passive understanding, being particular for each, disappears at man's death' (PPL 554, G vi 529).

analytical geometry
The application of the symbolic language of algebra to analyse and solve the problems of geometry. This branch of geometry was largely invented by Descartes. See his *Geometry*, appended by Descartes to his *Discourse on Method* (1637) together with his *Optics* and *Meteorology*.

a parte rei
Literally 'from the side of the thing', this Scholastic phrase embodies the assumption that true propositions have a basis in an independent reality.

a priori
a priori knowledge, as opposed to that which is *a posteriori*, is independent of experience. Leibniz held that all God's knowledge is *a priori*, including His knowledge of contingent truths (see *Discourse* §13).

arché
A Greek word meaning origin or beginning, used by some ancient Greek philosophers to signify an original principle that continues

to govern the working of the universe and by seventeenth-century vitalists like Robert Fludd and Henry More to signify a spiritual principle required for the explanation of natural phenomena. As Leibniz's own system could have struck his readers as vitalist — in the *New Essays* he claims his system makes sense of 'those who put life and perception into everything' (p. 72) — he found it important to dissociate himself from what he regarded as the anti-scientific features of vitalism (see *Discourse* §11 and *Supp.* 14).

Averroism

Averroes was a twelfth-century Arab scholar whose commentaries on Aristotle were highly influential and controversial in the Christian world up to and during the Renaissance. In continuing to make so much of opposing Averroism, Leibniz reveals his concern with the defence of individual immortality. The Averroists believed that the world is animated by a single spirit and that, after death, souls merged into it like streams into the ocean. Leibniz's opposition to this view is connected with his opposition to *quietism.

Cartesians

Those who adopted and attempted to apply what they took to be the main ideas of René Descartes in scientific method and philosophy. Leibniz tended to accuse them (see *Discourse* §17) of following Descartes slavishly and failing to do original work on their own. He at one time included Spinoza in a list (PPL 94, G i 16) of Cartesians but removed it on reading a book by Spinoza that confirmed his originality. In that spirit he never classified either Malebranche or Arnauld as Cartesians and, indeed, sometimes contrasts their views with those of the Cartesians. It is likely that in later life Leibniz came gradually to realise that he had not been entirely fair in dismissing the Cartesians as mere disciples. Amongst those whom he read were Johann Clauberg (1662–5), who introduced Cartesianism into Germany, as well as Louis de la Forge (died *c.* 1679) and Geraud de Cordemoy (died 1667), who were among the *occasionalists (see *Supp.* 6).

catoptrics

That part of the science of optics that deals with reflection at mirrors.

complete (being or concept)
A complete or perfect concept of something is one whose possession would allow a deduction of all the predicates that are true of the subject in question. A complete being is a true individual, i.e. a being whose complete concept is different from that of any other being (see *Discourse* §8).

concurrence (of God)
A phrase from Scholastic theology intended to denote the way in which God allows, but yet is not the cause of, human actions. A theory of concurrence, such as that offered by Leibniz, is intended to solve the difficulty of how, if God is omnipotent, things happen in the world that do not accord with His will. In the *Discourse*. or so he believed, Leibniz had a way of solving this difficulty. (See *Discourse* §7)

'connection of things'
A phrase Leibniz often used (e.g. *Discourse* §8) to refer to one consequence of God's wisdom, namely, that in choosing to create any given individual substance He had regard to His plans for the whole universe and therefore for all other substances. See also under 'sequence' and 'order' and *Supp*. 18.

continuum
A continuum is anything that is extended in space or time but is not divisible into real parts. One of Descartes's critics, Libert Fromond (1587–1653), wrote a book on the labyrinth of the composition of the continuum. The problem was how any continuum could be real if any of its parts was further sub-divisible. Leibniz inferred from this that space and time were not real things (*Supp*. 19) and nor would matter be if, as Descartes alleged, its essence consisted of extension alone (see *Discourse* §12).

Deus ex machina
A phrase used in drama where the playwright has failed to find a plausible resolution of the plot and has resort to the intervention of a deity. Leibniz was critical of philosophers who had resort to God's agency in matters he believed should have a natural explanation. The system of *occasional causes was, he thought, open to this criticism.

differentiae
A term of Aristotelian logic denoting the characteristic attributes that distinguish a particular species from other species of the same genus.

dioptrics
That part of the science of optics that deals with the refraction of light, or the bending of light that occurs when it is transmitted through different transparent objects such as glass prisms, lenses, etc. (see *Discourse* §22 and *Supp.* 10).

efficient cause
See under 'final cause'

emanation
A Neoplatonist doctrine, probably orginating with Plotinus (205–70), according to which the world is continuously produced by a kind of overflowing of the Divine Intelligence. Leibniz invokes the doctrine, in *Discourse* §§14 and 32, likening emanation to the way that thoughts are produced by our minds. Leibniz's commitment to this doctrine is marginal and he does not enlarge on what would be involved on his version of it. It is reasonable to suppose, however, that emanation would be a result of God's perfection (see *Discourse* §5) and that therefore his own version of it would not be the same as that of Plotinus.

Ens a se
Scholastic phrase meaning, literally, 'being by itself', something whose existence is not conditional on the existence of anything else. God's *aseity* involves the thought that He is a necessary being in contrast with contingent beings (see *Discourse* §23).

ens per se
Literally 'a being through itself', i.e. a being in its own right having a genuine identity of its own, as opposed to being possessed of a merely accidental identity. Elsewhere Leibniz talks also of an *unum per se*, a being with a genuine unity as opposed to one with a merely accidental unity, such as a flock of sheep or a pond of fish. See *Supp.* 7.

essence
A Scholastic term. Whatever is part of the *definition* or the *concept* or the *nature* of something is part of its essence (see, for instance, *Discourse* §§13 and 14).

ex hypothesi
Literally, 'from the supposition'. A logical term used in hypothetical reasoning to draw attention to the fact that some statement follows from what has already been supposed rather than to claim that it is true in itself. Leibniz distinguished between what was necessary as a consequence of God's primary decrees (*ex hypothesi*) and what was necessary in itself or absolutely, independently of these decrees (see §13).

expression
One thing 'expresses' another, in Leibniz's special sense of this term, when there is a constant and regular relation between what can be said of the one and what can be said of the other. In this sense an ellipse can be said to 'express' a circle, since every point on each has a counterpart on the other. (See *Supp.* 8 for Leibniz's own fuller explanation of the term and Introduction, Section 2.4 above, for an account of the relation between the notion of expression and other Neoplatonic notions defended in the *Discourse*.)

extent (of the soul)
Leibniz frequently alludes to the 'extent' of the soul (e.g. *Discourse* §§27 and 29) but does not always make clear what he means. His meaning is made clear, however, in §15 where Leibniz claims that substance 'is of an infinite extent in so far as it expresses everything'.

'extrinsic denomination'
A Scholastic phrase used to refer to cases where the basis on which something is predicated of something else does not lie in the thing itself. It is contrasted with an 'intrinsic denomination'. Leibniz denied that there were any purely extrinsic denominations (see *Supp.* 19).

final cause
One of Aristotle's four kinds of 'cause' but contrasted particularly in seventeenth-century debates with 'efficient cause'. Final cause

explanations are purposive in character whereas efficient cause explanations are not. Descartes had claimed (see *Supp*. 14) that natural science should use only efficient casues. Leibniz argues repeatedly (e.g. *Discourse* §§ 17–22) against this. (See also *Supps*. 9 and 10.)

forms
See under 'substantial forms'.

inesse
Leibniz attached a good deal of importance to the principle that in every true proposition the concept of the predicate is included in the concept of the subject. In a letter to Arnauld he went so far as to describe it as 'my fundamental principle' (G ii 56). See Introduction, Section 4 above.

influence (influx)
The theory that causal interactions between different substances consist in an *influxus physicus* was owing to Francisco Suárez (1548–1617) and seems to have been widely accepted by Scholastic philosophers in the seventeenth century. Leibniz was severely critical of inventing technical terms to give the appearance of solving problems:

> On the invention of this ... word Suárez prides himself not a little. The Scholastics before him had been exerting themselves to find a general concept of cause, but fitting words had not occurred to them. Suárez was not cleverer than they, but bolder, and introducing ingeniously the word *influx*, he defined *cause* as *what flows being into something else*, a most barbarous and obscure expression. (PPL 126, G iv 148.)

innovator
The charge of 'innovation' was made against those who were too eager to put forward views that went against established opinion. This charge was particularly made against those philosophers whose views had implications for orthodox theology. It was made against Leibniz himself by Arnauld on the strength of his synopsis of the *Discourse* but it was a charge Leibniz fervently repudiated:

> ... I want Mr Arnauld to realise that I make no claim to the glory of being an Innovator, as he seems to understand my views. On the contrary I usually find that the oldest and most generally accepted

opinions are the best ones. And I think that one cannot be accused of being an Innovator if one merely produces certain new truths, without overturning established opinions ... (G ii 20f.)

Jansenists
A Catholic sect who thought of themselves as followers of Augustine, named after Cornelius Jansen (1585–1638). The Jansenists included some distinguished philosophers amongst their number, including Blaise Pascal (1623–62) and Antoine Arnauld (1612–94). Leibniz had another reason for being interested in the Jansenists, that their outlook shared a good deal in common with the Lutherans. This may be one reason why he regarded Arnauld as a good person to approach in beginning his scheme for reconciling the Catholics with the Lutherans. In fact, however, the Jansenists were regarded as subversives by the French authorities even in Leibniz's time and were persecuted to extinction in the eighteenth century.

lowest species
A lowest species is one which is uniquely determined by the concept or definition that is given for it. If 'man' is defined as a 'rational animal', to take one of Leibniz's examples, the question whether man (so understood) is a lowest species turns on whether or not there are other rational animals of whom things are true that are not true of humans. (Leibniz discusses this in his *New Essays*, pp. 400 ff. and elsewhere.) Each individual is a lowest species, in this sense, if every other individual is in some respect different, i.e. if there are no two individuals that are exactly alike. (See *Discourse* §9.)

mechanical philosophy
The view that nature should be understood, as the workings of a machine (such as a clock) were, exclusively in terms of *efficient rather than *final causes.

middle knowledge (*scientia media*)
A phrase introduced by the sixteenth-century Spanish Jesuit Luis Molina in a book purporting to reconcile human freewill with divine foreknowledge and predestination. Leibniz took an interest in the controversy sparked off by this book, giving an account of it in his *Theodicy*. (See extract in *Supp.* 13.)

mirror

The metaphor of a mirror was a favourite with Christian Platonists. In his *System of Theology* Leibniz elaborates on the passage from St. Paul (I Corinthians, 13:12) by saying:

> ... in every state of our existence, our mind is a mirror of God and of the universe; with this difference, that, in the present state, our view is clouded, and our knowledge confused. When, therefore, this cloud shall be withdrawn, and when God shall manifest Himself more clearly, we shall see God face to face, and we shall see all other things (as we do even now) in Him as the medium ... (Russell, ed., 1850, p. 73).

In *Discourse* §9 he wrote that every substance was both a mirror of God and of the universe. But his considered view was that only minds are mirrors of God. The view that all substances are mirrors of the universe is one Leibniz develops through his theory of *expression.

Modern philosophers

Leibniz sometimes uses this phrase to refer to seventeenth-century philosophers generally and sometimes more precisely to refer to those philosophers who denied the Scholastic doctrines of 'general natures' and 'substantial forms'. The more precise sense appears to derive from the *via moderna* of the nominalists (following William of Occam) who, according to Leibniz, held to the rule that 'everything in the world can be explained without any reference to universals and real forms' (PPL 128). In a writing of 1670 Leibniz endorsed this rule and added that 'nothing is more worthy of a philosopher of our own time' (PPL 128). This more precise use is to be found in *Discourse* §8, the vague use in §3. See Introduction, Section 2.2. above.

nominal (definition or explanation)

Merely verbal. Contrasted with a *real* definition or explanation. See *Discourse* §14.

occasional causes

Leibniz, in common with Malebranche and a number of the *Cartesians, denied that there was any causal interaction in the world, strictly speaking. The occasionalists maintained, however, that only God was a true cause and that, for example, God makes our arms move on the 'occasion' of our willing them to move. Leibniz objected to this because it involved denying action to creatures (*Discourse* §8, see also *Supps.* 6 and 15). See Introduction, Section 3 above.

order
Leibniz held that the universe was fundamentally orderly but distinguished between those aspects of 'the general order' human beings could understand (those governed by natural laws) and those they could not. Miracles are departures from the natural order, according to Leibniz, but not from the general order (see *Discourse* §7). Leibniz, like Malebranche (and perhaps following him), frequently uses the phrase 'the order' to refer to 'the general order'.

paradox
As used by Leibniz, a dialectical term which was intended to indicate that a claim being put forward is contrary to the best authorised opinion and hence that the onus of proof lay with the person putting it forward. Leibniz himself accepts this onus in relation to the paradoxical consequences of his theory of substance (see *Discourse* §9). Elsewhere he is dismissive of paradoxical claims that are put forward without adequate substantiation. We have a right to *presume* a paradox to be false until it is proved true. (See *New Essays*, p. 517.)

passion
'Passion' in the sense followed by Leibniz stands to 'action' as 'passive' stands to 'active' and does not have such additional connotations as being overtaken by emotion.

perfection
In 1676 Leibniz had defined a perfection thus: 'By a *perfection* I mean every simple quality which is positive and absolute or which expresses whatever it expresses without any limits' (PPL 167, A II i 271).

Peripatetics
A name given to a school of philosophers for whom Aristotle's authority was overriding. The name was applied abusively by the Modern philosophers to the *Scholastics.

phenomena
Our 'phenomena', according to Leibniz, are 'all that can ever happen to us' (§14). His thought is that the universe consists in 'the general system of the phenomena' of the substances God has seen fit to create (§14). Each would have just the phenomena it has, even if there was nothing else in the universe but it and God. Nonetheless, there is a correspondence between the phenomena of different substances so that 'what is peculiar to one' becomes 'public to all' (§14). 'Phenomena' thus tends to be a theory-laden term in Leibniz's use in which the emphasis is on what happens to or how things appear to individuals, though it sometimes occurs (e.g. §§17–19) with its familiar public overtones, meaning what is observed or even what happens (§30).

the Philosophers
This is a reference to what was still the dominant philosophy in seventeenth-century universities, namely that of the *Scholastics. Leibniz often refers to Scholasticism as 'the common philosophy'.

Platonists
Leibniz's regard for Plato was probably greater than for any other philosopher and this regard extended also to some of the Platonists, including Plotinus (205–70 AD). A number of Leibniz's distinctive doctrines, for instance, his view that substances are indivisible and indestructible, that minds are 'images of divinity' and that 'every mind contains a kind of intelligible world within itself' are amongst those he acknowledges as 'Platonic' (see, for instance, PPL 592). But Leibniz would have refused the label 'Platonist' and, although he was clearly influenced in many ways by the Platonists, he is often at pains to distance himself from their tendency to prefer spiritualised explanations to scientific ones (see under arché) and the tendency of some of them to *quietism. See Introduction, Section 2.3.

quietism
A mystical doctrine according to which the soul should seek to achieve a state of tranquillity by surrendering its desires and purposes to the will of God. A renewed interest in the controversy about quietism was aroused by the publication, in 1675, of Miguel de Molonos's *Spiritual Guide*. The quietists were suspected both

of fatalism and of denying the individuality of souls by suggesting that they are 'absorbed in God' after death (see PPL 594). Leibniz thought Descartes' philosophy encouraged quietism. (See *Supps.* 3 and 9, compare *Discourse* §4.)

requisite
A Scholastic term. One thing is a 'requisite' of another in this sense if the existence of the first is needed for the second to exist.

Scholastics
Scholasticism was a label applied to the dominant style of University philosophy in the seventeenth century. Among its hallmarks was a reverence for Aristotle and a tendency to make the practice of philosophy subservient to religion. For Leibniz and other 'Modern' philosophers the doctrine that was especially associated with the Scholastics was that of *substantial forms. (See *Discourse* §10 and Introduction, Section 2.1 above.)

sequence (of things)
Leibniz refers variously to the sequence (of things), the order (of things) and the connection (of things) when he wants to emphasise the fact that there is a reason in God's plan why each event takes place which has to do with how it is connected with all the others. See also under 'order' and 'connection'.

species (messenger)
The Scholastic theory of perception, according to which objects transmitted something of themselves or something resembling themselves to us in virtue of which we can see them, was regarded by Leibniz and other Moderns as both obscure and gratuitous. Malebranche devoted a short chapter of his *The Search after Truth* (Book III, Part II, Ch. 2) to sketching how 'the least mental effort' would yield an inexhaustible number of objections to this view. Their rejection of such influences was common ground between Malebranche and Leibniz. (See *Supp.* 12.)

Spinozists
Followers of the Dutch Jewish philosopher Benedict Spinoza (1632–77) whose metaphysics Leibniz saw as a development from that of Descartes. In his *Theodicy* (Preliminary Dissertation §9)

Leibniz alludes to a compatriot, J. P. Speth 'who taught under the name Moses Germanus, having adopted the dogmas of Spinoza'. But it is not clear whether in using the label Spinozist (in *Discourse*, §2) Leibniz had anyone in particular in mind. Followers of Spinoza, unlike followers of Descartes, were hard to find in the late seventeenth century and it is possible that Leibniz used the label 'Spinozist' for those who developed Descartes's thoughts, if only privately, in the direction of Spinoza. (See *Supp.* 9 for a revealing account of what Leibniz wanted to resist in Spinoza's doctrines.)

Stoicism
A philosophy deriving from Ancient Greece and revived at various times. The fashion for Descartes's philosophy was partly due to its Stoic ethical content to which Leibniz was hostile (see *Supps.* 1 and 4). Leibniz was later to claim, however, that his system preserved 'the Stoic connectedness' in a way that made it compatible with spontaneity and therefore free will (see PPL 496). His use of the phrase 'connection of things' as a variant on 'the order' or 'the sequence of things' in the *Discourse* suggests that he wished even then to signal a willingness to accept Stoicism in part, without its fatalism.

subaltern
In scholastic philosophy, things were first classified into general heads and these in turn were subdivided into less general *subaltern* heads until in the limit the *lowest species was reached. Once defined, each classificatory head was though to be the subject of a deductive science, so that the sciences based on subaltern heads became subaltern sciences based on subaltern norms. It suited Leibniz to appeal to this hierarchical ordering of concepts and sciences.

substantial forms
Characteristically Scholastic notion intended to denote that in virtue of which something is an individual substance of a certain kind. According to those Scholastics who believed there are natural kinds or essences in nature, each kind of thing has a separate substantial form by reference to which its peculiar characteristics are to be understood. The use of substantial forms in attempting to

explain particular phenomena was regarded by the Moderns, including Leibniz (see *Discourse* §9), as obscurantist. Leibniz, however, held the view of the nominalists that the only real things were individuals and not kinds. By holding that each individual is a *lowest species, the way was open for him to make use of the notion of a substantial form as equivalent to the individual nature of a substance, as analogous therefore to a soul and indeed, in the case of humans and animals, as identical with the soul.

'Suppositum'
Scholastic term meaning 'substantial individual'. In a work of around 1668 Leibniz wrote:

> An entity which subsists by itself is the same as what the mass of Scholastics mean by *suppositum*. For a *suppositum* is a substantial individual ... Moreover, the School has generally established it as a property of *suppositum* that it is itself denominated by action; hence the rule that actions belong to *supposita*' (PPL 117, A VI i 511).

This rule is expressed in the Latin dictum: *actiones sunt suppositorum*, invoked by Leibniz in *Discourse* §8.

Supralapsarians
Leibniz deals at much greater length with the origin of sin in his *Theodicy*, where he refers to the supralapsarians as 'writers who maintain that God, wishing to manifest his mercy and justice in accordance with reasons worthy of Him, but unknown to us, chose the elect, and in consequence rejected the damned, prior to all thought of sin, even of Adam, that after this resolve He thought fit to permit sin in order to exercise these two virtues, and that He has bestowed grace in Jesus Christ to some in order to save them, while he has refused it to others in order to be able to punish them' (§82). Leibniz's own account allowed him to give a good sense to this view and so to claim (*Discourse* §30) that it is no more difficult to accept than other views.

system
Used broadly, a theory or organised body of knowledge, in science, metaphysics or theology and, more strictly, a well-organised set of principles and hypotheses. The *Discourse* is itself the presentation of a system but in it the only references to systems are to those in

natural science (§§5 and 21) or to the universe conceived as an interconnected whole (§14). Leibniz refers in his notes on the Malebranche-Arnauld controversy to 'my system' (see *Loemker* (1946, p. 465) but it is not till the 1690s — particularly with the publication of his 'New System of the nature and communication of substances' — that he makes much reference to his philosophy or anyone else's as a system. The reason for this has probably to do with an increasing fashion in French philosophical circles for using the word '*système*' of bodies of philosophy like that of Malebranche and an increasing interest — indicated, for instance, by Pierre-Sylvan Regis's *Système de philosophie* (1690) – in how such works ought to be organised. It is only in his later writings that Leibniz shows an overt interest in what a philosophical system should be like.

term
In a technical (logical) sense a term is one of the items related in a proposition. Hence 'subject-term'. (See *Discourse* §8.)

Thomists
Followers of Thomas Aquinas (1224–74), who thought his writings achieved an unrivalled accomomodation between Christian and Aristotelian thought. In the sixteenth century, Thomists enjoyed a high peak of activity in Spain and it seems to have been Spanish scholastic theologians (see *Supp.* 13) of whom Leibniz himself used the label 'Thomist'.

Bibliography

I Editions of Leibniz's writings

(a) Original language editions

Couturat, Louis (ed.), *G. W. Leibniz: Opuscules et fragments inédits de Leibniz*, Paris, 1903.

Deutsche Akademie der Wissenschaften (eds.), *Sämtliche Schriften und Briefe*, Darmstadt and Leipzig, 1923. Definitive but far from complete edition. (Referred to above as 'A', followed by series, volume and page number.)

Dutens, Louis (ed.), *God. Guil. Leibnitii ... Opera Omnia*, Geneva, 1768.

Gerhardt, C. I. (ed.), *Mathematische Schriften von G. W. Leibniz*, 7 vols, Berlin and Halle, 1849–60. (Referred to above as 'GM'.)

Gerhardt, C. I. (ed.), *Philosophische Schriften von G. W. Leibniz*, 7 vols, Berlin, 1875–90, republished Hildesheim and New York, 1978. (Referred to above as 'G' followed by volume and page number.)

Grua, G. (ed.) *Textes inédits*, Paris, 1948.

Le Roy, Georges (ed.), *Leibniz: Discours de Métaphysique et Correspondance avec Arnauld. Introduction, texte et Commentaire*, Paris, 1957.

Lestienne, Henri (ed.), *G. W. Leibniz. Discours de Métaphysique*, Paris, 1907. New edition with introduction by A. Robinet, Paris, 1983.

Lewis, Geneviève (ed.) *Lettres de Leibniz à Arnauld, d'après un manuscrit inédit, avec une introduction historique et des notes critiques*, Paris, 1952.

Robinet, A., *Malebranche et Leibniz*, Paris, 1955.

(b)   English language editions

Alexander, H. G. (ed.), *The Leibniz-Clarke Correspondence*, Manchester and New York, 1956.

Farrar, Austin (ed.), *Theodicy. Essays on the Goodness of God, the Freedom of Man and the Origin of Evil*, trans. E. M. Huggard, London, 1951.

Loemker, L. E. (ed.), *Gottfried Wilhelm Leibniz: philosophical Papers and Letters*, (2nd edition) Dordrecht, 1969. (Abbreviated above as 'PPL'.)

Lucas, Peter G. & Grint, Leslie (eds), *Leibniz. Discourse on Metaphysics*, Manchester, 1953.

Mason, H. T. (ed.), *The Leibniz-Arnauld Correspondence*, Manchester, 1967.

Remnant, P. & Bennett, J. (eds), *G. W. Leibniz: New Essays on Human Understanding*, Cambridge, 1981. (Referred to above as *'New Essays'* and by the page-number of the Akademie edition indicated by Remnant & Bennett in the margins of their edition.)

Russell, C. W. (ed.), *A System of Theology*, London, 1850.

Wiener, P. (ed.), *Leibniz: Selections*, New York, 1951.

II   Primary Literature

This a list of primary texts referred to in this edition, including some of Leibniz's own publications and sources used or alluded to be Leibniz in the *Discourse* or in the Supplementary Texts. We have given English titles of works available in a modern English edition.

Aristotle, *Metaphysics*, many editions, (4th Century BC).

Arnauld, Antoine & Nicole, Pierre (1662), Dichoff, J. & James, P. (trans.), *The Art of Thinking*, Indianapolis and New York, 1964.

Arnauld, Antoine, *Des Vraies et des Fausses Idées contre ce qu'ensigne l'auteur de la recherche de la vérité*, Paris, 1683.

Bosse, Abraham, *Manière universelle de Mr. Desargues pour practiquer la perspective par petit-pied, comme la geometral . . .*, Paris, 1648.

Cordemoy, Geraud de, *Le discernement du corps et de l'âme*, Paris, 1666.

Descartes, René (1637), Paul J. Olscamp (trans.), *Discourse on Method, Optics, Geometry and Meteorology*, Indianapolis, 1965.

Descartes, René (1644), Miller, R. P. & Miller, V. R. (trans.), *Principles of Philosophy*, Dordrecht, 1983.

Fludd, Robert, *Philosophia Moysaica*, London, 1638. (Translated by Fludd into English in 1659.)

Foucher de Careil, A., *Nouvelles lettres et opuscules inédits de Leibniz*, Paris, 1857.

Foucher, Simon (1675), Watson, R. A. (ed.) *Critique de la Recherche de la Vérité*, New York and London, 1969.

Foucher, Simon, *Réponse a la Critique de la Critique de la Recherche de la Vérité sur la Philosophie des Academiciens*, Paris, 1679.

Foucher, Simon, *Dissertation sur la recherche de la vérité, contenant l'apologie des academiciens*, Paris, 1687.

Froidmont, Libert, *Labyrinthus, sive de compositione continui*, Antwerp, 1631.

Heliodorus of Larissa (2nd century AD?), Bartholinus, Erasmus (ed.), *Damiani philosophi Heliodori larissaei de Opticis libri duo*, Paris, 1657.

La Forge, Louis de, *Traité de l'esprit de l'homme*, Paris, 1666.

Leibniz, G. W., *Theory of Abstract Motion*, 1671, (PPL 139ff; G iv 228ff.)

Leibniz, G. W. 'Unicum opticae, catoptricae et dioptricae principium', *Acta Eruditorum*, 1682, (*Dutens* III 145ff.).

Leibniz, G. W., 'A brief demonstration of a notable error of Descartes and others concerning a natural law', *Acta Eruditorum*, 1686, (PPL 296–301, GM vi 117–19).

Leibniz, G. W., 'A new system of the nature and communication of substances', *Journal des Savants*, 1695, (PPL 453–9, G iv 477–87).

Locke, John, 'An examination of P. Malebranche's opinion of seeing all things in God', in *Posthumous Works of Mr John Locke*, 6 vols, London, 1706.

Malebranche, Nicolas (1674–5), Lennon, T. M. & Olscamp, P. J. (trans.), *The Search after Truth*, Columbus, 1980.

Malebranche, Nicolas (1680), Dreyfus, G. (ed.) *Traité de la nature et de la grâce, Oevres Complètes*, Vol. V, Paris, 1980.

Malebranche, Nicolas (1688), Ginsberg, Morris (ed. & trans.), *Dialogues on Metaphysics and on Religion*, London, 1923.

Molina, Luis de, *Liberi Arbitrii cum Gratiae Donis, Divina Praescientia, Providentia, Praedestinatione et Reprobatione Concordia*, Lisbon, 1588.

Molinos, Miguel de, *Guida Spirituale*, Rome, 1675.

Molyneux, William, *Dioptrica Nova: Treatise of Dioptrics*, London, 1692.

Plato (early 4th century BC), *Phaedo* and *Meno* (many editions).

Spinoza, Benedict, *Ethics*, included in his *Opera Posthuma*, 1678, many editions.

von der Vorst, Conrad, *Tractatus theologicus de Deo*, 1610.

III Secondary Literature

(a) Works referred to

Aiton, E. J., *Leibniz: A Biography*, Bristol and Boston, 1985.

Broad, C. D., 'Leibniz's *Predicate-in-Notion principle* and some of its alleged consequences', *Theoria*, vol. XV, 1949, reprinted in Frankfurt (ed.), 1976, pp. 1–18.

Brown, Stuart, *Leibniz*, Philosophers in Context Series, Brighton, 1984.

Brown, Stuart, 'Leibniz's break with Cartesian "rationalism"', in Holland (ed.), 1985, pp. 195–208.

Costabel, Pierre (1960), Maddison, R. E. W. (trans.) *Leibniz and Dynamics*, Paris and London, 1973.

Couturat, Louis (1902), Ryan, R. A. (trans.), 'On Leibniz's metaphysics', 1972, in Frankfurt (ed.) 1976, pp. 19–45.

Frankfurt, Harry G. (ed.), *Leibniz: A Collection of Critical Essays*, Notre Dame and London, 1976.

Heinekamp, A. (ed.), *Leibniz et la Renaissance*, Wiesbaden, 1983.

Holland, A. J. (ed.), *Philosophy, its History and Historiography*, Dordrecht, 1985.

Kulstad, Mark (ed.), *Essays on the Philosophy of Leibniz*, Rice University Studies, Vol. 63, No. 4, 1977.

Loemker, L. E., 'A note on the origin and problem of Leibniz's discourse of 1686', *Journal of the History of Ideas*, 1947, pp. 449–66.

MacDonald Ross, George, 'Leibniz and Renaissance Neoplatonism', in Heinekamp (ed.), 1983.

Nason, J. W. (1942), 'Leibniz and the logical argument for individual substances', *Mind*, vol. 51, 1942. Reprinted in Woolhouse (ed.) (1981), pp. 11–29.

Osler, Margaret J., 'Eternal truths and the laws of nature: the theological foundations of Descartes' philosophy of nature', *Journal of the History of Ideas*, Vol 47, 1985.

Papineau, David, 'The *vis viva* controversy', *Studies in History and Philosophy of Science*, 8, 1977, pp. 111–42. Reprinted in Woolhouse (ed.), 1981.

Parkinson, G. H. R., *Leibniz on Human Freedom*, Wiesbaden, 1970.

Radner, Daisie, 'Is there a problem of Cartesian interaction?', *Journal of the History of Philosophy*, 23, 1985, pp. 35–49.

Schmitt, Charles, *Studies in Renaissance Philosophy and Science*, London, 1981.

Woolhouse, Roger (ed.), *Leibniz: Metaphysics and Philosophy of Science*, Oxford Readings in Philosophy, Oxford, 1981.

(b)   Other sources and writings recommended for further study of the Discourse

Adams, R. A., 'Leibniz's theories of contingency', in Kulstad (ed.), 1977, pp. 1–41.

Beck, Lewis White, *Early German Philosophy: Kant and his Predecessors*, Cambridge, Mass., 1969.

Broad, C. D. (1948–50), Lewy, C. (ed.), *Leibniz: An Introduction*, Cambridge, 1975.

Collins, Arthur W., 'The Unity of Leibniz's thought on contingency, possibility and freedom" in *Thought and Nature: Studies in Rationalist Philosophy*, Notre Dame and Indiana, 1985 Ch. IV.

Hacking, Ian, 'Individual substance', in Frankfurt (ed.), 1976, pp. 137–53.

Hooker, M. (ed.), *Leibniz: Critical and Interpretive Essays*, Minneapolis and Manchester, 1982.

Leomker, L. E., 'Leibniz's doctrine of ideas', *Philosophical Review*, 1946, LV, pp. 229–49.

MacDonald Ross, George, *Leibniz*, Past Masters Series, Oxford, 1984.

McRae, Robert '"Idea" as a philosophical term in the seventeenth century', *Journal of the History of Ideas*, 26, 1965, pp. 175–190.

Russell, Bertrand, *A Critical Exposition of the Philosophy of Leibniz*, London, 1900.

Sabra, A. E., *Theories of Light from Descartes to Newton*, London, 1967. Republished Cambridge, 1981.

Scheffler, Samuel, 'Leibniz on personal identity and moral personality', *Studia Leibnitiana*, 8, 1974, pp. 219–40.

Westfall, Richard S., *The Construction of Modern Science: Me-*

chanism and Mechanics, New York, 1971. Republished in Cambridge History of Science Series, Cambridge, 1977.

Woolhoose, R. S., 'The nature of an individual substance', in Hooker (ed.), 1982, pp. 45–64.

Index of names

Index of subjects

action   17, 33, 45f., 53f., 77f., 97,
  100f., 124f., 135f.
    immanent vs *transeunt*
      100f., 141
anatomy   43
animals   49f., 52, 62, 65, 81, 86,
  139
a priori vs *a posteriori*   22f., 46,
  50f., 66, 68f., 113, 129, 132f.,
  *143
a parte rei   55, *143
arbitrary   12, 26, 39f., 107, 113 *see
  also* voluntarism
arché   15, 48, 122, *143
astronomy   43
atheism   11, 24
atoms   79, 102, 136f.

best   31, 63f., 73, 120
    of all possible worlds   74
    see also perfect(ion)
bodies *see* substance(s), material

catoptrics   65f., 109, *144
cause   20, 54f., 57, 63, 65f., 136,
  148
    efficient   9, 15f., 65f., 97,
      108f., 123, 145, *146, 149
    final   9, 12, 15, 61f., 65f., 95,
      97, 105f., *147f., 149
    first   /9
    occasional   10f., 29, 77, 99,
      131, 136, *159

secondary   15, 86
Supreme   106
universal   77f., 107, 135
censor   2, 91
Christian   9, 12f., 24, 144, 151 *see
  also* orthodoxy
clear and distinct (ideas or
  knowledge)   23, 29, 35, 56, 113f.
common sense   5
communication (of substances)
  11, 17, 20, 29f., 34, 54f., 77, 101
    see also mind–body problem
complete (concept or notion)   20,
  27, 46, 50f., 54, 74, 76, 86, 129,
  134, *145
concomitance *see* harmony,
  pre-established
concurrence (of God)   15, 45, 48,
  57, 72f., 120, 135, *145
confused (perceptions)   78
    of the universe   51, *145
connection *see* harmony; order
conspire ('all things ...')   127, cf.
  79
contingent (vs necessary)   28, 50f.,
  96f., 133, 161
continuum   48, 137, *145
contradiction (principle of)   119,
  130, 132f
corporeal substances *see*
  substance(s), material
correspondence *see* harmony,
  pre-established

Spr 91
|
Vac 93
|
Spr 94
|
Spr 95
|
Sum 96
Vac 96
|